Editor-in-Chief and Founder:
  Lyndon H. LaRouche, Jr.
Editorial Board: *Lyndon H. LaRouche, Jr. , Helga
  Zepp-LaRouche, Robert Ingraham, Tony
  Papert, Gerald Rose, Dennis Small, Jeffrey
  Steinberg, William Wertz*
Co-Editors: *Robert Ingraham, Tony Papert*
Managing Editor: *Nancy Spannaus*
Technology: *Marsha Freeman*
Books: *Katherine Notley*
Ebooks: *Richard Burden*
Graphics: *Alan Yue*
Photos: *Stuart Lewis*
Circulation Manager: *Stanley Ezrol*

INTELLIGENCE DIRECTORS
Counterintelligence: *Jeffrey Steinberg, Michele
  Steinberg*
Economics: *John Hoefle, Marcia Merry Baker,
  Paul Gallagher*
History: *Anton Chaitkin*
Ibero-America: *Dennis Small*
Russia and Eastern Europe: *Rachel Douglas*
United States: *Debra Freeman*

INTERNATIONAL BUREAUS
Bogotá: *Miriam Redondo*
Berlin: *Rainer Apel*
Copenhagen: *Tom Gillesberg*
Houston: *Harley Schlanger*
Lima: *Sara Madueño*
Melbourne: *Robert Barwick*
Mexico City: *Gerardo Castilleja Chávez*
New Delhi: *Ramtanu Maitra*
Paris: *Christine Bierre*
Stockholm: *Ulf Sandmark*
United Nations, N.Y.C.: *Leni Rubinstein*
Washington, D.C.: *William Jones*
Wiesbaden: *Göran Haglund*

ON THE WEB
e-mail: eirns@larouchepub.com
www.larouchepub.com
www.executiveintelligencereview.com
www.larouchepub.com/eiw
Webmaster: *John Sigerson*
Assistant Webmaster: *George Hollis*
Editor, Arabic-language edition: *Hussein Askary*

EIR (ISSN 0273-6314) *is published weekly
(50 issues), by EIR News Service, Inc.,
P.O. Box 17390, Washington, D.C. 20041-0390.
(703) 777-9451*

European Headquarters: E.I.R. GmbH, Postfach
Bahnstrasse 9a, D-65205, Wiesbaden, Germany
Tel: 49-611-73650
Homepage: http://www.eirna.com
e-mail: eirna@eirna.com
Director: Georg Neudecker

Montreal, Canada: 514-461-1557

Denmark: EIR - Danmark, Sankt Knuds Vej 11,
basement left, DK-1903 Frederiksberg, Denmark.
Tel.: +45 35 43 60 40, Fax: +45 35 43 87 57. e-mail:
eirdk@hotmail.com.

Mexico City: EIR, Sor Juana Inés de la Cruz 242-2
Col. Agricultura C.P. 11360
Delegación M. Hidalgo, México D.F.
Tel. (5525) 5318-2301
eirmexico@gmail.com

Canada Post Publication Sales Agreement
#40683579

Postmaster: Send all address changes to *EIR*, P.O.
Box 17390, Washington, D.C. 20041-0390.

Signed articles in *EIR* represent the views of the
authors, and not necessarily those of the Editorial
Board.

Release
The 28 Pages!

In the Wake of Paris: Release the 28 Pages Now!

by Jeffrey Steinberg

Nov. 17—On Jan. 7, 2015, just hours after terrorists staged an assault on the Paris offices of the satirical publication *Charlie Hebdo* and killed a dozen people, former U.S. Senator Bob Graham (D-Fla.) joined House of Representatives Members Walter Jones (R-N.C.), Stephen Lynch (D-Mass.), and Thomas Massie (R-Ky.), and representatives of the 9/11 families, in a Capitol Hill press conference, convened to demand the immediate release of the 28-page chapter from the original 2002 Joint Congressional Inquiry into 9/11, which documented the role of the Saudi Royal Family in financing the hijackers.

Sen. Graham's words are even more profound and timely today, in the wake of the Nov. 13 Paris massacres by Islamic State-allied butchers. Graham told the standing-room only crowd:

> The Saudis know what they did. They are not persons who are unaware of the consequences of their government's actions. Second, the Saudis know that we know what they did! Somebody in the Federal government has read these 28 pages, someone in the Federal government has read all the other documents that have been covered up so far. And the Saudis know that.
>
> What would you think the Saudis' position would be, if they knew what they had done, they knew that the United States knew what they had done, and they also observed that the United States had taken a position of either passivity, or actual hostility to letting those facts be known? What would the Saudi government do in that circumstance, which is precisely where they have been for more than a decade?
>
> Well, one, they have continued, maybe accelerated, their support for one of the most extreme forms of Islam, Wahhabism, throughout the world, particularly in the Middle East. And second, they have supported their religious fervor, with financial and other forms of support of the institutions which were going to carry out those extreme forms of Islam. Those institutions have included mosques, madrassas, and the military. Al-Qaeda was a creature of Saudi Arabia; the regional groups such as al-Shabaab have been largely creatures of Saudi Arabia; and now, ISIS is the latest creature!
>
> Yes, I hope and I trust that the United States will crush ISIS, but if we think that is the definition of victory, we are being very naive! ISIS is a consequence, not a cause—it is a consequence of the spread of extremism, largely by Saudi Arabia, and if it is crushed, there will be another institution established, financed, supported, to carry on the cause.
>
> So the consequences of our passivity to Saudi Arabia, have been that we have tolerated this succession of institutions,—violent, extreme, extremely hurtful to the region of the Middle East, and a threat to the world, as we saw this morning in Paris.

Sen. Graham was absolutely right on Jan. 7. His words now take on even greater significance, as the entire world is still in shock over the Friday events in Paris, and the prospect that it can happen again.

It Can Happen Again

ISIS has already issued a new threat of similar blind terror attacks, this time targeting Washington, D.C. and other American cities. The Russian government, after a careful investigation, has concluded, as of Nov. 17, that the Metro Jet plane that blew up over Sharm el-Sheikh, Egypt, was downed by a terrorist bomb planted on board. ISIS has claimed credit for that atrocity, in which 224 people were killed. ISIS also took credit for a pair

White House/Pete Souza

President Obama and Saudi King Salman during the arrival ceremony for Obama in Riyadh, January 27, 2015.

Time for a Reckoning

Congress must not tolerate one more moment of White House cover-up of those 28 pages. The Joint Inquiry was a legislative branch investigation, and the Congress has total authority to release the 28 pages, whether the White House goes along or not. The 1971 U.S. Supreme Court unanimous ruling in the case of then-Senator Mike Gravel (D-Alaska), who placed the Pentagon Papers into the Congressional Record under the "speech and debate" clause of the Constitution, makes clear that Congress has the Constitutional authority to declassify those pages immediately.

While it is known that those pages provide details of how the Saudi General Intelligence Directorate supported at least two of the 9/11 hijackers upon their arrival in California, and how then-Saudi Ambassador to the United States Prince Bandar bin-Sultan provided funds to the two hijackers, the pages clearly contain other vital details and leads on the full scope of the Saudi regime's backing for the 9/11 killers.

Had the full scope of the Saudi Monarchy's bloody hands behind 9/11 come out at the time, no American President could have gotten away with the coddling of the Saudis that has been the hallmark of both the Bush and Obama Administrations, post-9/11. To this day, President Obama openly praises the Saudis for their role in the "coalition" fighting ISIS. Even if he had committed no other impeachable acts, this President's shameless coverup of the Saudi hand behind global jihadist terrorism, itself rises to the threshold of "high crimes and misdemeanors" that warrant immediate impeachment proceedings.

If there is to be any justice for those who died in 9/11, who perished aboard Metro Jet, who were brutally murdered in Paris and in southern Beirut, the full complicity of the Saudis must be exposed publicly, now.

Otherwise, as Sen. Graham so presciently warned, Al Qaeda and ISIS may be formally crushed, but the underlying disease will resurface in a new and more virulent form in no time at all.

Release the 28 pages now!

of suicide bombings in southern Beirut on Nov. 12, which killed and wounded hundreds of innocents.

Sen. Graham is absolutely right. ISIS is a consequence of Saudi promotion of Wahhabism and violent jihadi terrorism. To be more precise, Al Qaeda, the Islamic State, the Nusra Front and other terrorist groupings are products of an Anglo-Saudi alliance, most publicly associated with the Al Yamamah arms-for-oil barter deals between London and Riyadh. Al Yamamah created an offshore slush fund for terrorism that directly fed Al Qaeda, from the start of that sinister deal in the 1980s.

The shock of the Paris attacks has forced the Obama Administration, for the moment at least, to abandon its hate campaign against Russia and President Putin, and at least formally accept the urgency of collaboration with Moscow to crush the Islamic State.

Now it is time for a reckoning with the Anglo-Saudi apparatus that has been steering the growth of the global jihadist apparatus, through decades of funding and logistical support.

It is time to release the full 28 pages from the Joint Congressional Inquiry into 9/11. The release of those 28 pages should be the start of a thorough, top-down investigation into the role of the Saudi Monarchy in promoting global terrorism, starting with full disclosure of the Saudi role in the Sept. 11, 2001 attacks on the World Trade Center and the Pentagon.

EIR Contents

www.larouchepub.com Volume 42, Number 46, November 20, 2015

Cover This Week

Beirut, Lebanon, November 12, 2015.

Beirut, Lebanon Nov. 12, 2015

Ratib Al Safadi/Andolu Agency

LaRouche: To Save Civilization, Place Your Voice!

Editted excerpts from a talk by Lyndon LaRouche to associates on Nov 10, 2015.

We are now in the process of moving our organization as a whole into the area of Manhattan; which is where it should have remained always, according to Alexander Hamilton's intention. What we're getting now is, we're moving rapidly. First of all, we are clearing up the question of music. We no longer accept mere music; it's a failure, it's a mistake, because it has no placement of the voice; and the basis of everything depends on the placement of the voice. Otherwise, you really don't have a basis of unity. When people use different terms, different words, idiosyncrasies and so forth, and try to make that set of idiosyncrasies and trade styles into a nation, that was always a failure; that was always an error.

And what we're seeing now, which I began to put into effect in October of 2014, my intention from that point on has been to eliminate that kind of system among the states; which is a change that must occur if the competence of the United States is to be brought into being.

Now what's happening, we've taken the placement of the voice, the true placement of the human voice,

picture by Ricardo André Frantz

A segment of Luca della Robbia's choir loft (Cantoria) from the Renaissance Florence cathedral (Duomo).

which is not a snarl or a growl or a coughing up of things; but it's a way which is not mathematical. Mathematics is the enemy of the human mind; it always has been. And the point is that mankind's creative powers, the placement of the voice as such, is the principle of organization of a competent society. And that's where we are now; it's coming on fast. We're not getting all the results we would like to get immediately, but they're coming on fast.

And we're going to accelerate this continuously, because the principle is the placement of the voice, and you have a model of this in the case of Furtwängler's work. Furtwängler's work fits precisely into that question of the placement of the human singing voice. And what we're doing is, we're re-assembling our organization in that area; not just in Manhattan, not just in the New York organization, but in the surrounding area. We are now creating a new kind of understanding of what the United States always was intended to be. And now we're going to have to make it come to be what it always should have been, advocated by Alexander Hamilton and such people as that.

So the point is, the use of music is legitimate as long as you don't sing the wrong way. Your voice has to be placed appropriately; you don't make sounds, you understand the principle of musical composition. And you work at maintaining that. We have a fairly enthusiastic bunch of people who are assembling around us in the Manhattan area and around that; and this thing is developing rapidly. This defines the true meaning of what the United States should have always represented. And the "blab, blab, blab," and "blab, blab, blab," and all those kinds of funny sounds will have to be purged.

And it's working in the Brooklyn region where we're working; it's going to work. It takes time to adjust the pianos and other instruments; it takes time to bring a concert of the instruments into the right configuration which conforms to the principle which we call the Italian principle.

Conductor Wilhelm Furtwängler with the soloists for a performance of Beethoven's Choral Symphony (the Ninth) in Bayreuth in 1954.

And the idea is, get rid of local states. Filling stations are allowed; but otherwise, we don't want local states. We want a state; and a state which will be in harmony hopefully with other states. But the United States is a single state; it is not a collection of states. And that was always true—as Alexander Hamilton had already argued—and the United States has never worked successfully, except as a single nation.

It has to be a single nation with a single quality of singing voice; and that's what we're working on. We're working on that standpoint of reference as a scientific principle; and to bring everything into conformity with the proper placement of the human singing voice. And the instruments will also be told to behave.

We are on the point that this whole system, the whole United States system in its present form, is ready to disintegrate. And the only way you're going to prevent a disintegration is by learning to place your voice properly. And that's the law; and it's being worked on at this moment, as you sit here. That's happening right now in the fringes of Manhattan; that's where we're going. Why are we going there? Because it doesn't make a damn bit of good not to do it. And that's what our project has to be.

We're at a point of real desolation of all hope of mankind under the present global conditions. There are parts of China, parts of India, some other parts; but in the trans-Atlantic region, we have essentially degeneration. Not a regeneration, but a degeneration; and I think

it will not hurt anybody to find themselves placing the human singing voice. It would take a little work on some parts, but it's the principle that makes the difference. The old habits don't work; they never did. But when you have the proper placing of the voice by people who are properly directed musically, then you have something.

The Voice Seems Not to Sound

The point is—the thing to always go back to: You never sound music. You don't sound the music as such; you place the voice. And the placement of the voice creates the music. It is not your throat driving some kind of machine that makes noises; it's the idea of the placement of the mind.

And the best example of that, of course, for modern purposes of practice, is Furtwängler: Furtwängler's notion of the placement of the voice. Now this is not unique to him, but the emphasis, shall we say, on the question is very strong; there's nothing that matches it. You see other things in the musical domain which have the same thing; you don't sound the notes. You create the activity of the voice; and there's a difference, a fundamental difference. And therefore the idea in the Italian model, which is the Classical Italian model, is the most efficient standard model.

Now Helga and I, in our various occasions in Italy, working with the Italian music people and forces,—that's what they did, and the placement is there. If you go to the Italian performers of that generation—our generation—the placement is there. You do not make a sound; that's not music. You make a vacuum in a sense, which is the voice. You resonate something in that sense; you don't generate a noise. You place the voice. And that term "place the voice;" and the most exacting kind of placement is Furtwängler. Furtwängler is the actual measure of what the principle of the voice is.

And we have people who are practicing as musicians, and they work on the basis of the placement of the voice; not the voice as such, but the placement of the voice. The placement of the voice is what's important. And anyone who has a beautiful voice, has it essentially because of placement; and that placement is what's crucial. That placement is what makes the meaning of "human" pleasant. And that's the truth of the matter, and it is rarely understood very well.

And I have had the opportunity of living in Italy at various points during my whole career. And with the Verdi commitment, which is the best; it's the best we have in general knowledge in modern experience. And the best of the Italian singers: they live to make music; and they understand what that means. They free their voice of garbage and litter; and they let the voice speak for itself. The voice does not sound apparently; it does not have a sounding character; it captivates people because it is not a form of noise. It involves the question of placement; placement above all.

And I know there are people in this room who have some knowledge of this matter. But don't fall into the trap of singing jazz.

Why Are They All So Stupid?

People have the simplistic conception of the sound of the voice as such, and things like that, as the principle of human behavior; that is not true. The characteristic is, and the music is, that the music itself, the musical voice as such is the standard. Not the decorations, not the noises, not anything else. It's the placement of the voice, and the placement of the voice is not something that you generate physically. It's not that way. What it is, is the character of the mind.

Now, for example, what's wrong with the average citizen of the United States today? Just the average citizen. Why are they all stupid? What is their stupidity? They believe that they make noises; they talk, they make noises; they rub, they make noises. This has nothing to do with mankind, but quite the contrary. The idea of placement of the voice is not making a sound. The placement of the voice is an act which has an effect; but it's not a noise. It's not a sound; it's not noise as such. It has a very specific kind of character, and any attempt to imitate that character without the right placement, is a failure.

Now, what's the result of the failure? Well, most people are stupid; most modern people are stupid. Why are they stupid? Because they don't have a placement of the mind. And the placement of the mind is not a noise; it's not a sound as such. And it's exactly what Furtwängler defined it to be, exactly that. That concept of placement of the voice. And art and so forth, the idea of physical art,—physical this, physical that,—that is not the point. That has an effect, and the effect has an implication; but the point is the placement of the voice. The voice is *placed*; it is not sounded. It is placed by tuning, the tuning of the voice.

And that's where the problem is. Because the question is here: What's important, making noises? Well, we can get skunks to make noises. As a matter of fact, skunks will make noises.

A Place which is No Place

The tuning principle we're organizing in Manhattan now, is a complete overhaul of the idea of music relative to what the standard has been heretofore for a long period of time. The placement of the voice is not something that's arbitrary. The placement of the voice is a particular area of the human mind, and the human mind's behavior, which responds to the human mind itself.

So, it's not tuning something; it's not tuning an object. The problem is most people tune objects. They don't tune the mind, they tune objects. What we're doing now in Manhattan, is we are now in a mass mobilization, relatively speaking, in Brooklyn and other areas, where we're working with people who are actually in the Italian school of placement. And placement is not something you can deviate from, and it's not a sound! It's a resonance, it's not a sound. And if you want to get the effect, the audible effect, you have to tune your mind to go to the right tuning.

Your mouth, your mind does not control music, not really, not under the Italian school. The placement of the voice, the exact *pitch* of the voice, that pitch is what your contract is; that pitch, the placement of that pitch. And you have to let it project. You don't utter it. You don't actually utter it; you cause it to be brought forth. And for example, the best example of that, the one that's most easy to see—look precisely at what Furtwängler did in his work. There's no such thing as tuning to a music that you impose. No such thing! It's a noise.

It's the placement of the voice, and the placement is

The New York Community Chorus rehearsing under the baton of Diane Sare.

a vacation—it's a place which is not a place. And you move, you become tuned. *You* become tuned. How? By placing your voice; but you don't make the voice. You hear the voice, but you don't make it. But you act in such a way as to respond, to resonate, with the voice that cannot be heard as such *per se*; not generated *per se*. It's the *placement* of the sound, but it's not the sound itself. And the placement authorizes the application of what you call the amplitude of the sound.

But it's not amplitude as such; it's the amplitude of the tuning. It's what we have now in Brooklyn, for example, which we're going to take about a year or so to get the pitch, and we're going to take the whole instrumental structure of the Manhattan musical performance; we're going to tune *everything* according to the Italian standard, the true Italian standard. And all the instruments, and the voices, and the voices are not spurting out noises,—they're receiving something, they're resonating, they are *tuned into the environment* in which they're speaking; they're tuned into the environment of their expression. Not the expression, but the tuning into the environment. And, that's the difference.

And that's a subject which is almost lost, unknown, to most people in music today. They have no conception of what the placement of the voice means. And yet the greatest singers and composers, musicians as well, instrumentalists as well, all understood it.

What's happened is today's population has no comprehension of what the whole damned thing is about! And only a handful of people have any real conception of this.

A Sound Which is Not

The best thing is the Furtwängler standard. The most precise approach is Furtwängler. Because that is perfect. Furtwängler's conception of this is perfect; the Italian thing is perfect, because it is the tuning principle,—the tuning of the voice is restricted. You cannot impose a tuning on the voice. You have to follow and adapt to the voice. And you are compelled to be obliged to that; otherwise it doesn't work!

What it means, is that it's not the sound that's created; not the sound as such. It's the human being, the tuning of the *mind* of the human being! Not the tuning of the voice; it's the tuning of the mind. And the tuning of the mind, and the tuning of the function of the mind are one and the same thing. And if you don't have the right placement, that does not work. And that's what the problem is. And the best thing we have, the best training, is the performance of Furtwängler! And the Italian school, as such. That is perfect.

And what do you think we're doing in Manhattan now? We're cleaning everything up, we're changing all the instruments; we're tuning them. We're tuning up the people, based on this principle of tuning. And you don't make the sound. Your presence makes the voice; you obey the voice. You don't generate the voice, you obey it. And you learn to obey. The successful singer learns to behave well, according to those standards. And what comes out of the singer, is something which the singer just does, because they understand what they must do; they understand what they must let their voice do, and at what pitch, at what tuning, at what mode.

Italian soprano Mirella Freni (left) on stage in Barcelona in 1993, and American bass William Warfield at a Schiller Institute event in May 1994. Both were signers of the Institute's petition to return to the Verdi tuning.

Schiller Institute

And that gets lost, because people try to make sounds, and making sounds is the wrong way to go at it. And Furtwängler made it very clear: what you have in tuning, is you have a non-sound. That's the genius of it. It's not a sound; in other words it's not a sound projected by the voice of the singer or an instrument.

What you have, is you tune yourself to mankind; you tune yourself to humanity. You do not direct a sound as such; you get something that flows from around the singer's mind, and so forth. But it's not created as making a noise, or a sound as such. It's the tuning of the body, the tuning of the mind. And all of the good things that come out of that process are of that nature. And the Furtwängler model is perfect on this thing; and Furtwängler, of course, uses one method, you know, the Italian method. And that's how the best work was done.

You don't make a sound, you don't push a sound out. You resonate in a certain way. And you look at Furtwängler's performances, which are on record and so forth, these things demonstrate the principle precisely; and that's the only true principle of music: the placement of the voice which is not generated by a *push* from a voice. It's a vacuum area, it's an area where it seems almost like nothing.

And follow this stuff with Furtwängler's work: He never makes a sound as such. He places the voice, the placing of the voice. And the people who are good in their singing, will do that. They won't push a noise out. They will *tune*, they will tune the entire environment.

And that's what's been lost! And you get singers who learn to do it, but when they really do it well, they don't think in those terms; they think about projecting, they think about forming the effect. But it has to be *tuned* right. The human voice is tuned, it isn't making noise, it's tuned.

In other words, just imagine an area of sound, a fluid of sound: absolute, indefinite sound. Now what, in that indefinite sweep of sound *per se*,— what constitutes real music? The thing that stands out, *the vacuum*; the place that is different. And when the singer is trained, the voice is trained, the voice follows that rule. And the most perfect example of this was done in examples by Furtwängler, who laid down what is essentially the Italian school, the true Italian school, which is based on this: you, your body, everything about you, has now been tuned,—like water,—tuned. And when you're tuned, then you're in harmony with the universe. And the purpose of music is to find mankind's sense of harmony, of mankind in the universe.

They're Being Human

The Classical Italian artistic composition, that's the principle. But if you want to do the Italian model in the right pitch, the right focus, you have to follow this rule. You have to say, "No, I'm not making a sound, I'm tuning myself against an environment which is different." And the point is, it really is, when you think about it, you think about real musical performances,—and instrumental as well as vocal, otherwise, same thing; and that is where the mistake is made. It's like this whole thing about mathematics. Mathematics is shit, that's the best thing that can be said for it. Because that's all it is. And you know, I've known this, I've been steeped in this thing in Italy! And the Italian standard is there, but the perfect expression today to define this definition about how this principle works, is Furtwängler. The most precise. You get it also in other places, but the most precise thing for modern purposes is that.

And what we have, is we have the whole musical program we're running in Manhattan, and out of Manhattan, is all based on this. Everything you need, the instruments and the singers are being tuned, tuned according to law. And it's by inspiring people to accept being tuned in that sense that they become human, and don't make non-human noises any more.

This is something; it's well-known, but we're so corrupted by assuming that different styles and different kinds of things,— and all these things,— make a sound! And it actually is the non-sound that you want to hear. The non-sound that is different than all the sounds around you.

EIRNS/Stuart Lewis

A sextet at the Schiller Institute's May 1994 conference at the Howard University Rankin Memorial Chapel, for a Marian Anderson National Conservatory of Music Movement. From left to right: Rev. James Cokely, George Shirley, Detra Battle (largely hidden), Kebeme (Valerie Eichelberger), William Warfield, and Robert McFerrin.

All you have to do, is get into—you know, sing it! Singing and finding out the placement of the voice. And people who can place the voice will tend to understand that; they may use another word for it, they may use another term, they may get distracted. But what they are is they are *human*! And what they're doing is, they're being *human*. As opposed to people who ain't so human.

And the Furtwängler model is the perfect one. The more general model is the Classical Italian or the modern Classical Italian. That is the most convenient one, the Italian, and Furtwängler had that, and Schlusnus had much of those qualities in placement of voice. Take recordings of Schlusnus's songs, and you will get a lot of that, and you will recognize exactly how that works.

Beauty by Subtraction

It means something when it's something which is different, where you change the atmosphere according to a principle. And the Italian school, the best Italian examples are the best models to use for general purposes. But Schlusnus of course has a particular capability for this matter.

And the point is, the problem is that our minds don't function properly, because we're too busy trying to make noises, according to some principle. We don't realize that when you organize the process in the proper way, that's what makes life rich and good. The good Italian school is also other schools of the same thing; people sing: beautiful voices. People sing. Why do they sing? To impress something upon the environment? On the contrary! They sing to eliminate the noises. And the remainder after that deduction is music.

I have enjoyed beauty for many years,—not recently so much; I'm in no condition to be involved in the music business otherwise, practically. But I know about it, and I haven't forgotten about it. I know when it's right; I'm also very aware when it's wrong.

You make people happy by getting the dirt out of the atmosphere and creating a blank area, where there is no dirt. And that resonates, by subtraction, by eliminating noises. I've said this for a couple of weeks already on this thing; the emphasis on this question. But the placement of the voice is not adding something to the voice,—it's subtracting from the noise! That's what's beautiful: You subtract the noise. And that's what makes you dream well, and think well, and enjoy life, by getting rid of bad noise in all forms.

On Musical *Placement*

by Philip Ulanowsky

Nov. 8—Over decades, Lyndon LaRouche has made a point of strategically redefining a word or term common to one or another pertinent branch of knowledge. To such terms—including common sense, manifest destiny, negentropy, and (musical) mode—he has recently added *placement* with respect to the language of Classical music.

In each case, LaRouche has presented his redefinition as an irony, an ambiguity to be resolved in the mind of his reader or listener, not merely to broaden, but to elevate that individual's conception of the subject and of his or her own humanity. Throughout, these attempts to engage the mind of his audience on a higher plane, have shared the purpose of provoking a clearer, more beautiful appreciation of the science of creative human society. That society, itself, has been eroded virtually past existence by cultural degeneration over more than a century to date.

"Placement" has long had a meaning in vocal training, stemming from discoveries in the science of vocal production by Leonardo da Vinci and the Florentine school of beautiful singing—*bel canto*—which flowered in the Fifteenth Century Italian Renaissance and has at least survived through the present. It refers, in essence, to the means of using the voice optimally, minimizing tension and friction in the vocal chords and using the natural resonance in the various cavities of the head, in particular, to allow the freest, most well-projected quality.

This technical placement, within a naturally defined musical tuning, allows singers long careers (other considerations aside) by avoiding strains on the vocal apparatus which otherwise tend to shorten the life of the natural instrument. But, to what end? Countless orators and actors have studied and mastered the same subject; we find ourselves in a cultural wasteland nonetheless, in which each new generation comes into, *and accepts as normal,* an uglier, more bestial state of affairs in virtually every aspect of life. In a world besieged by war and terrorism, drug abuse, and social disintegration, can such an issue as placement have any significance?

The Sleep of Reason

The answer to this reasonable question, emerges from recognizing that words, logic, explanation—all fail in a society dominated by irrationality. One may

Francesco Goya's Capricho 43 (1797), captioned "The sleep of reason produces monsters."

recall from Spanish painter Francisco Goya's 1797-98 *Los Caprichos*—a series of about eighty polemical prints revealing the ugly "secrets" of his society at that time—Plate 43, titled, "The sleep of reason produces monsters," and captioned, "Imagination abandoned by reason produces impossible monsters: united with her, she is the mother of the arts and the source of their wonders." When words lose their power to communicate, great art may carry its audience to that higher conception of humanity needed to become its better self.

Never has that need pressed us with more urgency than now. An honest look at the world around us suffices to show those "impossible monsters" on every side—both outside and in. It is thus to the power of great art that we look for a means to educate ourselves in the inexpressible, and to the power of music above all.

Placement, in LaRouche's new casting, escapes the confines of technique, to embrace the power of music to inspire. Although its technical aspects play an essential role, vocal "plumbing," no matter how good, can not generate the ideas upon which the future of civilization depends. (Technical skill in art may impress, but cannot substitute for ideas; technique must serve the higher purpose.) At the same time, any music worthy to be called great never stems from notes, any more than great poetry stems from words. In both, the true subject is *unheard,* an inexpressible idea in the mind of the composer, to be communicated to the mind of another individual, present only as *that which generated* the poem or the musical score. It lies behind the words and notes; it is the necessity bringing them into existence as momentary, partial expressions of a higher, creating process.

LaRouche's new, ironic employment of *placement,* then, obliges the performer to submit every technical, as well as aesthetical, consideration to the service of communicating a composition's insightful, universal idea, rejecting any sensual effect, no matter how appealing, which does not contribute to the strongest possible evocation of that idea in the audience. Without every effort to concentrate this power of art, our society will remain in the clutches of the debased "entertainment" and the profoundly pessimistic view of humanity it engenders, that have allowed us to walk so far down the path of failed civilizations past.

The Italian Classical School

by Liliana Gorini

Liliana Gorini, of Milan, Italy, is the chairwoman of MoviSol, Il Movimento per i diritti civili e la solidarietà.

Nov. 13—According to the Italian school of bel canto singing, placement (in Italian, *impostazione,* putting the voice in the right place) is achieved by "activating simultaneously all resonating chambers" of the human body—chest, throat, and head. One speaks of the "chest voice" for singing low notes, in the first register, and of the "head voice" (*registro di testa*) for singing high notes, in the third register (starting on F-sharp for tenors and sopranos) mainly using the head resonance. We see it clearly in Luca della Robbia's bas-relief "La Cantoria" in Florence, in which children are singing in a choir, and some of them have an intense expression and tension in the *maschera* (around the eyes, the "mask"), which shows that they are using the head voice and singing in the third register.

A throaty voice is, by contrast, considered an unpleasant voice. Singing teachers in the tradition of the ancient Italian school of bel canto teach their students to use all of these resonances, and the human body becomes in this way a natural amplifier. That is why opera singers do not need microphones and can reach their listeners in very large opera houses, or even in the Arena of Verona, an outdoor opera house, without any amplification, while rock singers, who have no placement, have to almost eat the mike to be heard—even in the front row.

To channel the air up to the head voice, the bel canto singer needs support (*appoggio*), which means once again that from the diaphragm up to the head, the human voice is organized and focused like a concentrated laser beam, so much so that a great singer can break a light bulb with a high note, but the same note will not move the flame of a candle.

Verdi Baritone Cappuccilli

A great master of placement and support was Piero Cappuccilli, the Verdi baritone who participated in the first international conference on scientific pitch held in Milan, at the Casa Verdi, on April 9, 1988. Cappuccilli then provided the first example of how the right pitch (or Verdi tuning, A=432 Hz) is crucial, when performing Verdi operas, for achieving the color of the voice and register shifts intended by the composer. To demonstrate this, he sang a passage from Verdi's *Ernani* in both tunings, Verdi's (A=432 Hz) and today's.

Today's tuning varies from A=440 in the United States to A=448 in Berlin, Vienna, Florence, and Salzburg, according to reports to this writer from other famous singers who supported the Schiller Institute campaign to go back to the scientific pitch, such as tenors Luciano Pavarotti and Carlo Bergonzi.

Italian baritone Piero Cappuccilli in Giuseppe Verdi's opera "Simon Boccanegra."

The late Cappuccilli (1926-2005), a very good friend of Lyndon and Helga LaRouche, not only supported the Schiller Institute campaign for Verdi tuning, but also gave a master class in bel canto singing in Stuttgart, Germany, where he coached young conservatory students on how to sing and interpret Verdi. Once again, the question of placement was the key. Cappuccilli was famous for his very long phrases, twice as long as his colleague baritones; he once told me that he developed this capability thanks to his job as a diver in the Coast Guard in Trieste, his birthplace, before he started his career as a singer.

Of course, he also insisted on interpretation, since, as LaRouche indicates in the discussion published here, the mind is the source of the right placement, and it is the right interpretation which makes the difference between a decent singer producing a nice sound, and a true artist who is able to move his audience to tears.

Political Tuning

What is true for the human voice, is also true for a political movement. I believe Lyndon LaRouche is using the idea of placement as a metaphor for how a political movement should function. If in placement you "activate simultaneously all resonating chambers" to get a beautiful tone, in a political movement you have to simultaneously activate all locals, all chapters, and all activists in order to achieve the maximum result.

An example of this is our Glass-Steagall campaign. We have achieved results, including making Glass-Steagall the key issue of the U.S. 2016 presidential campaign, thanks to an international campaign on this issue, including the many letters of support for the Glass-Steagall bills in the U.S. Congress that we generated from members of Parliament in Italy and all over Europe. As chairwoman of MoviSol—LaRouche's movement in Italy—in my discussions with members of Parliament and conferences on this issue, I often showed the LaRouche PAC map indicating the many resolutions for Glass-Steagall approved by state legislatures, as a result of the mobilization of activists and other citizens in the various states.

In Italy, as all over Europe, many people are demoralized as a result of the economic crisis, and believe that nothing can be done to overcome it, and to shut down Wall Street and the City of London. Showing them that we are mobilizing simultaneously all over the world on this issue, was vital for remoralizing them, and activating them to send messages to their political representatives, nationally and locally, to demand that they introduce Glass-Steagall bills or resolutions.

As a result, we have eight such Glass-Steagall bills in the Italian Parliament, and four regional councils (corresponding to a state legislatures)—Tuscany, Lombardy, Veneto, and Piedmont—have approved a resolution for Glass-Steagall. Another good example of "placement."

Some Thoughts Derived from Nicolaus of Cusa and Friedrich Schiller on Lyndon LaRouche's Concept of Placement of the Singing Voice

by William F. Wertz, Jr.

Nov 14—Recently in discussing his Manhattan Project, Lyndon LaRouche emphasized the importance of placement of the human voice in singing as the principle of organization of a competent society. In developing this concept, he stressed that he is not talking about the sound that is created, but rather "it's the tuning of the mind of the human being" that is at issue. "You tune yourself to mankind; you tune yourself to humanity."

Moreover, he describes the correct placement of the voice as a "vacuum area, it's an area where it seems almost like nothing. You make people happy by getting the dirt out of the atmosphere and creating a blank area, where there is no dirt."

"The Little Children Being Brought to Jesus," an etching and drypoint by Rembrandt, done in 1647-1649.

What LaRouche is describing is a state of mind which is required not only on the part of the singer, but also of the composer, the conductor, and the audience which experiences a performance and must then go forth to organize mankind to regain its own humanity. Fundamentally, the issue is not a technical issue *per se*. Rather the issue is how to place your identity, so that your life and action cohere with the true creative mission of the human species as a whole.

To understand LaRouche's concept, it is helpful to consider this issue from the standpoint of Cardinal Nicolaus of Cusa (Cusanus, 1401-1464) and the German poet Friedrich Schiller (1759-1805).

In Harmony with the Logos

In all of his writings, Nicolaus of Cusa emphasizes that the only way that society can be organized competently is if all human beings realize their nature, as created in the living image of the Creator, by rising above sense perception and logical deduction to the level of creative reason. Only if all human beings are thus in harmony with the Logos or the Word can there be universal concordance (*Concordantia Catholica* (1433)).

In a short essay entitled, "On the Filiation of God" (1445), Cusanus wrote:

Filiation [becoming an adopted son of God—

wfw], therefore, is the ablation of all otherness and diversity, and the resolution of everything into one, which is also the transfusion of the one into everything. And this is the theosis itself.... Therefore, you must elevate yourself in profound meditation beyond all contrarieties, figures, locations, times, images, and contradictions, beyond othernesses, disjunctions, conjunctions, affirmations, and negations, because through the transcendence of all proportions, comparisons, ratiocinations into the pure, intellectual life, as the son of life, you are transformed into life.. ..

In other words, to become an adopted son of the Creator, as LaRouche has emphasized, one must free the mind of all the noise and dirt which obstructs creativity.

Such a state of mind involves searching for the Creator within oneself, which means rising to the level of the simultaneity of eternity. As Cusanus points out in his essay "On Equality" (1459), when one is being creative, one finds oneself between the temporal and the eternal, or what he refers to as "timeless time."

The soul sees also that it is timeless time. For it perceives that time is in transmutable being and there is transmutation only in time. It perceives therefore, that time is always other in the temporal. Consequently, it sees that the time in it, removed from all otherness, is timeless. Hence the soul also sees that it is not eternity, since it is time, although timeless.

In his essay "On the Not-Other" (1462), Cusanus again stresses that the Creator is not anything created, and yet the Creator is the cause of everything created. Therefore, the Creator, who is Not-Other, is, by self-definition, Not-Other than Not-Other, and at the same time anything which is created or other, is, by definition, Not-Other than other.

In "On the Hidden God" (1444), Cusanus makes the same point:

In the domain of all creatures, neither God nor His name is to be found. And that God escapes every conception rather than be affirmed as something, since as something that does not possess the condition of a creature, He cannot be found in the domain of creatures. Also one does not find the not-composed in the domain of the composed. And all names, which are named, are names of composition. However, the composed is not from itself, but rather, from that which precedes all composition. And although the domain of the composed and everything composed are through this that which they are, nevertheless, since it is not composed, it is unknown in the domain of the composed.

Thus, when one is being creative in the living image of the Creator (not-composed), one is not in the domain of the composed. The causality of a composition is not in the domain of the composed. When you have correctly placed your identity, you are located in timeless time; you are what Nicolaus of Cusa refers to in "On Learned Ignorance" (1440) as a "finite-infinite."

The Aesthetical State of Mind

In his *Letters on the Aesthetical Education of Man*, the German poet Friedrich Schiller develops the same concept of a well-tuned soul, in aesthetical, rather than explicitly theological terms.

For Schiller, the only means by which society can be organized to reflect the true nature of man (in light of the failure of the French Revolution), is for man to raise his individuality to that of the species through the aesthetical education of his emotions.

Like Nicolaus of Cusa, Schiller argues that "man carries the predisposition for divinity in his personality within himself." Therefore, like Cusanus, he regards man as a finite-infinite. As a finite (material) being, man is characterized by sensuous drives. At the same time, as a creature of reason, man has a formal drive to impose a conceptual and moral order upon the sensuous world. If the sensuous drive dominates, then society descends into savagery. However, if the formal drive dominates by merely negating the sensuous drive, then society is characterized by Draconian barbarism.

Schiller resolves the twin evils of the compulsion of nature and the compulsion of reason by identifying what he calls the play drive, the direction of which is to "annul the time in time, to reconcile Becoming with Absolute Being, alteration with identity." Man, according to Schiller, is truly free from the one-sided compulsion of nature and reason only when he plays, which is to say, when he loves.

Both in his essay "On Grace and Dignity" and in his *Kallias Letters*, Schiller develops the idea that "man must bring his desire and duty into connection: he should obey his reason with joy." Schiller describes this fusion as a "reciprocal action between the finite and infinite."

Schiller describes this state of mind as finding oneself "at once in the condition of highest rest and of highest motion, and there results that wonderful emotion, for which the understanding has no conception and language no name."

Steve Carr

The statue of German dramatist/poet Friedrich Schiller in Detroit, Michigan.

In Schiller's view, the condition of the human spirit before all determination is a passive determinability without bounds. This might be compared to the theological conception of *capax dei*. Schiller calls it an empty capacity. This empty capacity is initially passively determined by the senses and then actively determined by reason, which imposes limits on the sensuous drive. Through both of these processes, however, man loses his humanity.

The question is how to create a state of mind free of any particular determination. According to Schiller, the play drive restores man's humanity through the creation of an aesthetical determinability. Thus beauty is our "second creator."

Like LaRouche, who describes placement as a vacuum area which seems almost like nothing, Schiller writes:

In the aesthetical condition man is therefore *naught*, insofar as one pays attention to a single result, not to the whole capacity, and takes into consideration the lack of any particular determination in him. Thus one must recognize as completely right, those who declare the beautiful and the state of mind into which it transports our mind, in regard to *knowledge* and *inner conviction*, to be fully indifferent and unfruitful. They are completely right, for beauty gives absolutely no individual result either for the understanding or for the will, she realizes no individual, either intellectual or moral purpose, she finds no single truth, helps us fulfill no single duty, in a word, is equally inept to establish the character or to enlighten the head. Thus, the personal worth of a man or his dignity, insofar as these can depend only upon himself, still remains fully undetermined by aesthetical culture, and nothing further is achieved than that it is now made possible for him *on account of nature*, to make of himself, what he will—that to him, the freedom to be what he should be, is completely restored.

As Schiller explains, this aesthetical state of mind is not an empty infinity, but is to be regarded as a fulfilled infinity.

In this third "joyous realm of play," man is set free from everything which is called constraint. The fundamental law of this realm is *"to give freedom through freedom."*

Germany's Role at This Decisive Point in History

by Helga Zepp-LaRouche

Helga Zepp-LaRouche gave the following keynote to the national party congress of the German political party BüSo (Civil Rights Movement Solidarity), which she heads, in Berlin on Nov. 14, 2015.

Ladies and gentlemen, honored guests of the BüSo, I am very happy that you're here, because everyone can sense that we have arrived at a turning point in history.

Before I speak more about that, I would first like to express my deepest sympathy for the victims of the attack in France, and to the whole nation of France.

It is totally clear that the bestiality and barbarity of

EIRNS/Christopher Lewis
Helga Zepp-LaRouche at the BüSo national party congress on Nov. 14.

these terror attacks almost surpass imagination. The latest information is that there were 7 attacks; 137 people are dead, and approximately 280 wounded, many of whom are in critical condition. You have to ask yourself, where does this bestiality come from? What makes human beings act as if they are no longer human beings?

It has been only 10 months since a similar attack was launched on the French satirical magazine *Charlie Hebdo*. The same day, there was a public event in the Congress in Washington, D.C., where former Senator Bob Graham charged that the terrorist attack on *Charlie Hebdo* was the result of the fact that President Obama, and Bush and Cheney, had covered up the real

circumstances of the 9/11 attacks. In particular, he said, the famous 28 pages of the original Congressional Joint Inquiry Report had still not been released to the public, even to this day. This, despite the fact that Obama had promised the families to do so in his 2008 campaign.

These 28 pages are relevant because, as far as we know from the allusions of Congressmen, who have read this report, they concern the role of Saudi Arabia and its financing of the terrorists on 9/11. In addition, the former head of the American Defense intelligence Agency (DIA), Gen. Michael Flynn, said in an interview this year with Al Jazeera, that his agency had, in 2012, warned the White House, and Obama personally, that the shipment of heavy weapons from Benghazi, a city in Libya, to the so-called "good rebels" in Syria, would end up in the hands of an Islamic Caliphate. That was two years before ISIS declared itself the Islamic State. General Flynn stated that Obama not only ignored this advice, but knowingly pursued a policy that would lead to such an Islamic terrorist state.

We have to have this in the back of our minds, and we need an open debate on it, to put an end to the sources of terrorism. General Flynn has said that it was a conscious and deliberate policy. That is the issue the Bundestag and our government should discuss.

The Kill Policy

It was just made known this year that the Pentagon has spent around half a billion dollars to train 5,000 rebels in Syria for the war against President Assad. Then, it turns out that, after many months of such training, a total of four rebels were left on the side of the United States. All the others had gone over to ISIS.

This farcical policy has meanwhile been the subject for the satirical show "Die Anstalt." In that show there was a very funny segment, which was a takeoff on the schmalzy "Das Herzblatt (Blind Date)." On one side of a partition was the American President, and on the other side three hooded ISIS fighters. He had to choose his "sweetheart"—which one is the good rebel, which one is the bad, and which one will change from good to bad (joining ISIS), against whom he must make war.

These connections are clearly just below the surface of German consciousness, or else they would not have been presented in this broadcast.

A few weeks ago a second whistleblower surfaced, a second Edward Snowden, who released the so-called Drone Papers to Glenn Greenwald and his Internet site *The Intercept*, where they were published. These papers reveal the enormous extent of the Obama Administration's drone policy. The official policy is to draw up lists of suspects, who will then be killed by drones, without due process of law. What emerges from these documents is that an average of 90% of the victims are innocent civilians, including children—who were placed on new lists of suspects, *after the fact*, in order to create a rationalization.

Already, back in May 2012, the *New York Times* reported that, every Tuesday is "Terror Tuesday" in the White House. President Obama personally compiles a so-called "kill list," which is the basis for the drone strikes for the coming week.

The clear consequence is that we are not dealing here with just murder, but with *mass murder.* This fact alone—that the President of the United States is allowed to kill people in this way, without a legal trial and without representation by a lawyer or defense counsel—is sufficient grounds for an immediate impeachment under the U.S. Constitution, and even the application of the so-called 25th Amendment. Anyone who so violates human rights, surely doesn't have the mental and moral qualifications for the office of the U.S. Presidency.

The significance of the Drone Papers is similar to that of the Pentagon Papers for President Nixon. At that time, the Pentagon Papers were leaked by Daniel Ellsberg to Sen. Mike Gravel. These documents showed clearly that the official line, that the Vietnam War was a total success, was a lie, and specifically, that the infamous body-count policy of Defense Secretary Robert McNamara, who every day counted the dead bodies, was criminal. These papers were then read by Senator Gravel, who invoked a special constitutional procedure to do so, into the official Senate record, which later led to Nixon's downfall.

You have to fathom what this drone policy is. Back in 2012, the Stimson Center, as well as the Naval Postgraduate School in Monterey, Calif., and the Rand Corporation, produced an analysis concluding that the drone policy had exactly the opposite result from that intended. For every terrorist who was eliminated, ten, 20 or 30 new ones were recruited, because the rage over the injustice of the murder of civilians, and over the barbarous arrogance, with which it is carried out, increases hatred for the West immeasurably. Thus the drone policy functions like cutting off the head of a hydra—for each head chopped off, 13 new ones grow.

The German Role

On Nov. 7, a week ago, the *Süddeutsche Zeitung* published a long article on the extent to which the German authorities are helping the United States in its drone war. The German authorities supply the Americans with telephone and SIM card numbers, which are used for the attacks on the terrorists. The drone attacks do not target specific suspects, but anyone who happens by chance to be holding the cellphone in his hand. No one verifies that this is the person who is on the list. Nor does anyone check where the cellphone is located. Whether the alleged terrorist is just then in a children's hospital, or in a crowded market, doesn't make any difference at all.

The American military base in Ramstein, Germany plays a central role in these attacks. Several weeks ago, a hearing by the NSA investigation committee in the Bundestag heard the testimony of former drone pilot Brandon Bryant, who has become a kind of whistleblower, because he said that he could no longer morally tolerate killing people in this mechanistic way. He reported that a device is attached to the bottom of the drones, called Gilgamesh, a radio cell which locates all cellphones in the neighborhood of the drone. If the number of a suspect shows up, then this drone is launched against the holder of this cellphone.

Former drone pilot Brandon Bryant, during an interview with MSNBC's Democracy Now in October 2013, exposing the immoral character of the drone policy.

All German intelligence services, according to Bryant's testimony, are working with this program: the Militärische Abschirmdienst [Military (Counter-Intelligence], the Verfassungsschutz [Federal Office for the Protection of the Constitution, roughly comparable to the NSA], and the BND [Bundesnachrichtendienst, equivalent to the CIA]. Up until 2014, the Americans were even allowed to question refugees, even those with German *Tarnpapieren* [faked identity papers issued by the authorities], for as much information as possible about the country from which they came; about people they knew; and in many cases, this was then followed by drone strikes. Many times Americans, disguised as Germans, would also question these refugees without German officials present. The *Süddeutsche Zeitung* came to the conclusion that without German participation, the drone war would not be possible in this form.

Ramstein is the hub for drone attacks in the Middle East and Africa. It has also been reported that the Federal Prosecutor General is currently investigating whether a preliminary investigation could be opened on the basis of charges brought by victims of these drone-kill operations—for example, the son of a victim in Somalia. The possible charge is accessory to murder, since there is no state of war between America and Somalia, or between Germany and Somalia. Thus these drone attacks do not fall under the laws of war, but under criminal law.

The obvious conclusion from all these things is that this form of cooperation must stop immediately, and after this convention, with the consent of all of us, we will send a message to the German government to this effect.

The War Threat

This matter has further implications on which I would like to now elaborate. Let me make a preliminary observation. If you look at the whole strategic situation—those who are here know much about it, because we are one of the few organizations which deal with strategic issues at all—the most shocking element is the enormous discrepancy between the dimensions and complexity of the crisis, and the relative cluelessness, or rather, indifference, shown by a large part of the population. We are standing on the edge of a third world war; we stand on the edge of a new financial crisis which will overshadow by far that of 2008; but if you look at the news media, if you listen to the politicians, you hear practically nothing about it.

The media dictatorship, under which we, without a doubt, live, makes it very difficult for the ordinary citizens to put the picture together. There is almost no report in the German media—and I follow the news with a nearly scientific or clinical interest—which does not have a twist, a spin. Be it about Ukraine or Syria, about China, or the refugee crisis, the news coverage in Germany is always tendentious. From the politicians you only hear approved themes. Certain subjects are not mentioned at all, and the subjects which are on the "approved list," as it were, are always treated with a certain bias.

In addition, distractions from reality are enormous.

I have just come back from the United States, and I turned on the TV, although I normally don't watch TV. What do I see? The Bambi awards [an award issued by the Burda media conglomerate to celebrate "achievements" in German TV, along the same line of entertainment self-celebration as the Oscar awards in Hollywood]. The first song I heard was more or less: "We are

FIGURE 1

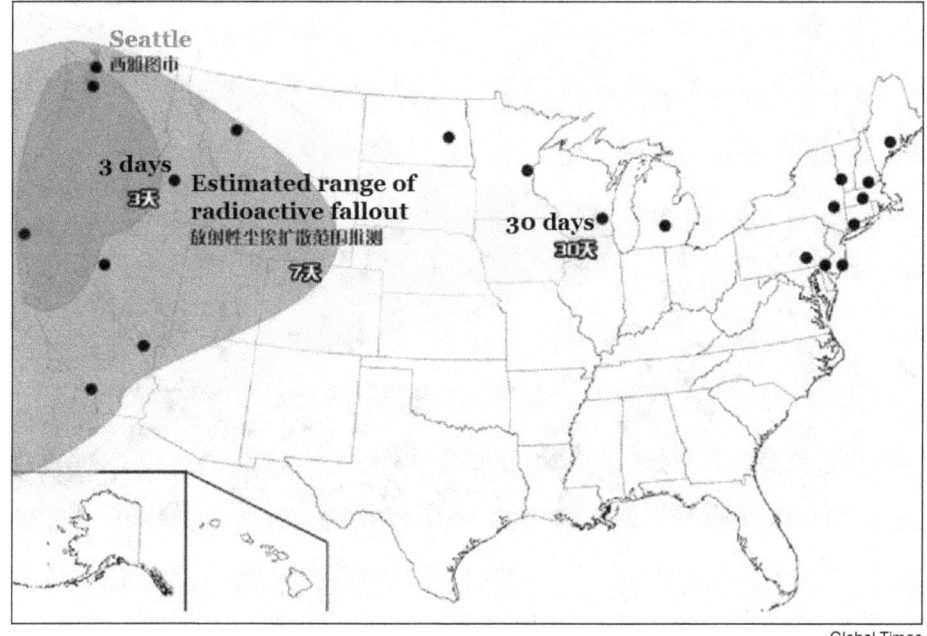

In October 2013 the Chinese paper Global Times published this grahic of the range of radioactive fallout which could hit the United States, if China were forced to respond to an attack by the West.

all going to die, we must live in the moment." The worst expression of the human spirit is the desire to live in the here and now, to forget everything else, and glorify the moment. That was the first concentrated message of this program.

The media are waging war against the population, by preventing people from thinking. There are rules of the game which you must follow. Whoever doesn't comply with the rules of the game, doesn't belong to the club, is ostracized. Whoever wants to belong to the "Western community of values," which is allegedly so superior to all other cultures, must abide by the rules of the game.

Of course, the war danger doesn't come from Russia and China, but from the policy of the Obama Administration and the British government. The reason for that is the continuity from the Bush Sr. Administration, an eight-year interruption with Bill Clinton, then eight years of the Bush/Cheney Administration, and now Obama; on the British side it was Thatcher, Blair, and Cameron. The common aim of these two countries is to create a world empire through the Anglo-American special relationship. This idea of creating a world empire, a unipolar world, has brought us toward a third world war. That is absolutely clear to Russia and China.

Putin's semi-annual meeting with Russia's military leadership has just taken place in Sochi. On Nov. 10, Putin stated publicly that Obama's policy boiled down to a nuclear first strike against Russia; that the missile defense system in eastern Europe isn't really about missiles from Iran or North Korea, but about the ability to disable Russia's nuclear second-strike capacity. This policy has been in preparation since the United Sates unilaterally withdrew from the ABM Treaty in June of 2002, under Bush Jr.

Since that time, Russia has had many conferences. At one security conference in Moscow three years ago, a video was shown from which it was very clear that the American BMD system in Poland, in the Czech Republic, in Romania, Bulgaria, and Spain, was not aimed against missiles from Iran, but it was meant to eliminate Russia's second strike capability. Putin made the point, which was obvious the whole time: that after the successful conclusion of the P5+1 agreement, where Iran agreed to renounce building nuclear weapons, and to accept to international controls, there is no longer any reason to continue building up this BMD system. It is exclusively about changing the strategic balance in favor of the United States and NATO, he said, and possibly winning a nuclear war.

The British paper the *Guardian* reported on Nov. 11, in an article by Julian Borger, on a PBS program on the modernization of American tactical nuclear weapons in Germany. The so-called B-61-12 tactical nuclear weapons, which are currently being modernized, have a modern tail kit with fins, more power, new electronics, a new explosive trigger, and a precision guidance, which allow them, when placed on a stealth bomber, to steal into the airspace of Russia, or other states, and not be observed by radar. The former commander of the American Nuclear Strike Forces, Gen. James Cartwright, said recently in an interview, that this modernization of tactical nuclear weapons in Europe—and Germany is one of the headquarters—makes the bomb more usable, and

Nirvana News

Xinhua/Peng Zhaozhi

Both Russia and China are actively upgrading their ability for self-defense. Here, we see Russia's latest intercontinental missile, the Bulava, being testfired in Nov. 2014, and Chinese nuclear missiles on parade in Beijing during the Sept. 3 commemoration of the end of World War II in the Pacific.

that there is a danger that, in this way, the world would slide into a third, this time nuclear, war.

That means that the old doctrine of Mutually Assured Destruction, of total obliteration of both sides—which meant a kind of nuclear balance of terror, because each side knew that it could not deploy nuclear weapons because the other side would do the same, and then there would be a total nuclear contamination of the planet, a nuclear winter that no one would survive—that this MAD doctrine no longer holds. On the contrary, some now think that the modernization of these nuclear weapons makes a first strike worthwhile, and that one could win a nuclear war.

The Russia-China Response

Russia and China have made it very clear that they are totally aware of this danger. At the military parade in Beijing on Sept. 3, on the occasion of the 70th anniversary of the end of World War II in the Pacific, China—and by the way, Putin was visible on the podium with President Xi the whole time—displayed a new missile which has a speed 10 times the speed of sound. It is assumed that it could be extremely dangerous for American aircraft carriers—that is, it can incapacitate them.

The Russian Navy has also undertaken tests of its Bulava missile from the submarine *Vladimir Mono-*

mak, in maneuvers that are to last until Nov. 16. The missiles arrived very precisely at the Kura test-site in Kamchatka. The U.S. Navy, on the other side, over last weekend, tested two Trident DS-missiles. In other words, we find ourselves in an arms spiral, where China and Russia are making it very clear that the idea of incapacitating their second-strike capacity with these modern weapons, is a total illusion.

The key lies with the submarines. If you realize how many thousand nuclear weapons are installed, partially on missiles, cruise missiles, aircraft carriers, submarines, moving trucks, and moving trains, it is perfectly clear that the idea of incapacitating the total second-strike capability of an enemy, is a total illusion.

The American military analyst Hans Kristensen, in a document well worth reading, has pointed out the fundamental difference between conventional and nuclear war. In a conventional war, one side will try with all its means to destroy the enemy's arsenal to the point that he can't fight any more, and then the war is over. In the case of a nuclear war, the idea that you can eliminate all the nuclear weapons is an illusion. The calculation assumes that it is not possible to do so, and that there are many possibilities of concealing them.

The Russian military budget amounts to approximately $49 billion today; the American military budget is 10 to 15 times higher. The United States has two new weapons systems in production—the F35 stealth airplane, and a new atomic submarine, both of which are more expensive than the entire Russian defense program. Sputnik News has reported that NATO is now preparing to take over the entire military and paramilitary establishment in Ukraine—that is, it will not pursue formal membership in NATO for Ukraine, but instead, full compatibility of the weapons systems and the command-and-control system is clandestinely in process.

U.S. Secretary of Defense Ashton Carter just came back from a trip to Asia, during which he launched an array of provocations. After that, at a press conference in the Reagan Presidential Library in California, he said that it is Moscow's saber-rattling which raises questions about the Russian leadership's commitment to strategic stability, and their respect for norms against the use of nuclear weapons, which leaders in the nuclear age have demonstrated in the past. He then issued a warning: "Make no mistake; the United States will defend our interests, and our allies.... We're investing in the technologies that are most relevant to Russia's provocations, such as new unmanned systems, a new long-range bomber, and innovation in technologies like the electromagnetic railgun, lasers, and new systems for electronic warfare, space, and cyberspace, including a few surprising ones that I really can't describe here."

It is not Russia which is making provocations, but Russia is reacting to exactly what Ash Carter has enumerated.

Fortunately, there is resistance in the United States—not yet a majority, but at least it's stirring. Democratic Congressman John Conyers, at the beginning of November, convened an event in the Congress, to which he invited members of the American Committee for East-West Accord, which is deeply worried about a new Cold War between the United States and Russia. Three members of this group all expressed their concern that the U.S. policy toward Russia has gone totally off the rails, and that the demonization of Putin, and the total disregard for Russian security interests and standpoint, have brought about a totally dangerous situation.

Former U.S. Ambassador Jack Matlock, who was the President Reagan's ambassador to Moscow at the time of the collapse of the Soviet Union, asserted there, once again, that at the end of negotiations with the Soviet Union, clear assurances had been given by the West, that NATO would not expand up to Russia's borders; that NATO could perhaps spread a protective umbrella over the states of the former Warsaw Pact, but would build no bases in these countries.

That is exactly what is denied by the media today. Matlock was an eyewitness—he was in Russia when Gorbachov was negotiating with then German Foreign Minister Genscher—and he has stressed this many times.

A specialist in Russian studies, Prof. Emeritus Stephen Cohen, from New York University, said that the new Cold War which we are now experiencing is much more dangerous than the old one. We have troops on the border with Russia, and there are no more rules of the game. Putin has reacted cleverly, he said, as a strategist, to all these things, and has created new facts on the ground through solid strategic cooperation with China. Whoever takes on Russia, must therefore assume that he will have to deal with Russia *and* China, and probably with a whole series of other countries.

Russia Turns the Flank

Above all, Russia, through its military intervention in Syria—which began on Sept. 30, has very rapidly created military facts on the ground, Cohen said, as the Russian Air Force is providing protection for the Syrian Army, which can then attack, and has made great progress against ISIS and other terrorist groups. But Russia has, at the same time, linked this with a global diplomatic initiative. It has brought all the countries of the region to one table.

The first meeting was two weeks ago in Vienna. Present were Saudi Arabia and Iran, two clear adversaries, but also Turkey, Jordan, and Lebanon. Today, the second Syria conference is taking place in Vienna. German Foreign Minister Steinmeier flew in for the meeting from Paris, where he was attending a soccer game, just as the terrorist attacks were being committed.

German policy clearly supports Russia's initiative fully, because it is the only chance for defeating terrorism. At this second conference today, according to my latest information, the Syrian government of Assad, as well as various rebel groups are participating. The objective is to reach a unity government, and eventually free elections in a transitional process—thus a political solution.

In response, the Obama Administration has sent 50 members of the Special Forces to Syria—the famous "boots on the ground"—an action which, under the

State Department

Russian Foreign Minister Sergey Lavrov with U.S. Secretary of State John Kerry in Vienna October 23, 2015. Their agreement has led to a series of fruitful negotiating sessions on Syria, involving more than a dozen nations.

U.S. Constitution, requires the consent of the Congress. Of course Obama has not gotten that approval. He is not in Syria at the invitation of the Syrian government, as Russia is, and he also has no mandate from the UN Security Council.

There is a bipartisan group in the U.S. Congress which has demanded an immediate debate and vote in Congress on this specific matter. It's represented by Rep. Jim McGovern (Mass.) on the Democratic side, and Rep. Walter Jones (N.C.) on the Republican side. Yesterday (Nov. 13), 35 more Congressmen demanded an immediate debate and vote on this mission in a letter to the newly elected Speaker of the House Paul Ryan. Under the United States Constitution, only the Congress, not the President, can decide whether to go to war. Obama has violated this principle many times, and that is also further grounds for impeachment.

Furthermore, the Pentagon has now confirmed that its provocations against China in the South China Sea will continue. Two B-52 bombers flew over the vicinity of a newly constructed Chinese island in the South China Sea, an action which was followed by an immediate warning from China, because the act violated Chi-

na's sovereignty. The *Global Times*, a Chinese paper close to the government, wrote that China is not afraid of a war with the United States. In the event military tensions in the Pacific between the United States and China intensify, China possesses weapons systems capable of reaching the territory of the United States. They made clear they will not capitulate.

When the ASEAN defense ministers met recently in Kuala Lumpur, Ash Carter tried to get this conference—of which the U.S. is not even a member, but had only been invited as a guest—to adopt American formulations on the tensions in the South China Sea; fortunately, it met strong resistance.

The United States had also tried, through subterfuge, to get the Philippines to allow U.S. military bases to be built on its territory, which is against the Philippine Constitution. The subterfuge it used was that it would station American weapons on Philippine bases, and still call them Philippine bases. The Philippine Supreme Court then ruled that this agreement did not constitute a treaty under international law, but was only an Executive order, and therefore the Senate did not have to ratify it. However, the Senate voted that it was a definitely a treaty under international law that the Senate had to approve. (See articles in Section III.)

So you see—and I can only cite a few examples here—that there is resistance throughout the world and many countries are aware of where it will lead.

What is the state of the resistance in Germany to these lunatic policies? Taking what I just now said, and what you, yourselves, know from the media or your own research—if you consider all of this, then I think it's absolutely time to reassess the strategic and existential interests of Germany, and define them anew. It can no longer be simply assumed that we are "a part of the western community of values," and that therefore, no matter what happens, we must always go along with what the United States and Great Britain present to us.

My husband, Lyndon LaRouche, who is an extremely acute strategic thinker, and has always put his finger on most critical elements, has recently referred to the fact that the United States has gone through a great change since the assassination attempt against President Reagan in the first year of his Presidency (1981). At that point, President Reagan fortunately was not killed, but he was nonetheless in a weakened condition, so that the influence of Vice President George Bush increased more and more. Especially during the last two years of Reagan's Presidency, he had increasing health problems, which dominated the situation.

Neo-Cons on the Rampage

Neo-con policies were continued when George H.W. Bush succeeded Reagan as President. Then there were eight years under Clinton, which were a mixture of good and bad, and then eight years of Bush and Cheney, followed by seven years of Obama. Thus, with an eight-year hiatus, we have had a continuity of neo-con policies in the United States for 21 years!

Department of Defense/Cherie A. Thurlby

President George W. Bush with his two chief advisors from PNAC, Defense Secretary Donald Rumsfeld (left) and Vice President Dick Cheney (right). The three are shown at Rumsfeld's farewell parade at the Pentagon in December 2006.

These policies had a massive influence on Europe. In 1997 an organization called the Project for a New American Century (PNAC) was founded in America. It's in this organization that the roots of the refugee crisis can be found. The members included Paul Wolfowitz, Richard Perle, Donald Rumsfeld, Dick Cheney, Robert Kagan—he's the husband of Victoria Nuland, a woman with a remarkable sexual drive, since she wants to f*** the whole EU; she must be a nymphomaniac of an extraordinary sort. At its founding this group said the United States must create a new American empire, and that was the policy which President Bush junior then pursued.

Unfortunately that was also the combination which dictated the situation when the reunification of Germany came about in 1989. We in Germany, especially the people of the former DDR, made a truly peaceful revolution. It was not only a "turning point," as the term was later modified into a circumlocution. It definitely could have been the beginning of a new order of peace for the Twenty-First Century.

Did Russia deploy tanks? Russia had agreed that German reunification would proceed peacefully and therefore had the justifiable hope that Germany would be a reliable partner, and maybe even a friend. The Russians are therefore tremendously disappointed and hurt that certain German governments have demonstrated themselves to be poodles of Washington and London. Then there were the Western concessions that there would be no NATO troops on the Russian border, which the Russians believed at the time.

The CIA did a study in 1991, which said that Russia's economic development should be discouraged, because Russia has more natural resources and a better-educated workforce than the West, and therefore any economic development would only result in Russia later becoming an even bigger competitor on the world market. So instead, Russia should be blocked economically. This then resulted in the famous shock therapy devised by various professors. From 1991 to 1994, this shock therapy reduced Russia's industrial potential by 70%.

The Russian economist Sergei Glazyev wrote in his book about the Yeltsin period of the '90s—which was appropriately titled *Genocide*—that this was a deliberate program of population reduction, in which the Russian population was reduced by about a million people each year. The mortality rate was higher than the birth rate.

This was also when the PNAC policy of regime change began: the Orange Revolution, the color revolutions in Ukraine, Georgia, and later in the Arab world, etc.

The consequence for Germany was that the achievement of German reunification, fully legitimate under domestic and international law, was betrayed because of the combination of French President François Mitterrand, who threatened German Chancellor Helmut Kohl with war, as Jacques Attali has reported in detail in his biography of Mitterrand; and British Prime Minister Margaret Thatcher, who at the time was reviling Germany as the Fourth Reich; and the elder Bush, who said that Germany had to be contained through self-containment. And the best way for this to happen was through German integration into the EU and the Maastricht Treaty—i.e., Germany had to give up the D-Mark, was forced into the European Monetary Union, and thus embedded or locked into this alliance.

Then came eight years of Clinton. These were a mixture. The Oslo Accord was good, but the neocons immediately came up with the "Clean Break" policy, so regime change was to be the policy for all the governments in the Middle East. Then in 1999, the Glass-Steagall Act was repealed, completely in the interests of Wall Street.

On Jan. 3, 2001 my husband gave a very famous webcast in which he said that the administration of Bush, Jr., which would be coming into the White House three weeks later, would confront with difficulties in the financial system far beyond what people imagine, and that they would therefore stage a new "Reichstag fire." That was exactly nine months before Sept. 11.

Sept. 11 was not at all what the official line says, and this is now a very hot topic in the American Congress, where about 21 Representatives and also some Senators are demanding the publication of these 28 pages. And of course the 3,000 family members of the World Trade Center victims have built a movement in America that is demanding the same thing. As many attest who have read these 28 pages, they have nothing to do with U.S. national security interests, but rather the cover-up of criminal machinations. This is something that must be made public.

If what happened on Sept. 11 was not what the offi-

LPAC/Matthew Ogden

Former Senator Bob Graham at a press conference on Jan. 7, 2015, where he demanded the release of the 28 pages in the interests of national security, as well as justice.

cial account describes, then, of course, the Afghanistan War, which was based on Article 5 of the NATO Treaty, is also invalid. And after all, this war is one of the reasons for the refugees. Today, there are millions of people who can no longer stay in Afghanistan, because the 13 years of NATO deployment there have only made everything worse. Drug production in Afghanistan is 40 times what it was before. That is one way that the terrorists are being financed. The Taliban is expanding its control, and the people are fleeing from these circumstances. Sept. 11 is therefore an important issue for the refugee question.

This was also, of course, the time of the extensive abrogation of civil rights in the United States, with the Patriot Act and various follow-up laws. Then the unbridled addiction of the NSA to investigating everything in the world that moves, to check out every e-mail, every phone call—it really is an addiction. There is no way that all of this data could be evaluated; it's a mania.

Wars Built upon Lies

The Iraq War that began in 2003, of course, is the result of the memorandum of British Prime Minister Tony Blair and the MI6, a memorandum riddled with lies, which then U.S. Secretary of State Colin Powell presented to the UN General Assembly as the reason for war: that Saddam Hussein possessed weapons of mass destruction that could reach every city in the world in 45 minutes—all that was a lie. That is another reason for the refugees: the war in Iraq.

In March 2011, support for the Opposition in Syria began in the context of the Arab Spring. The military attack on Libya in 2011, the brutal murder of Qaddafi—these are also reasons for the refugees. Today, if we look at Libya, the country is completely destroyed, razed to the ground. You don't have to be a friend of Saddam Hussein, or Qaddafi, or President Assad, but the fact is that these States, with these Heads of State, were functioning countries with a functioning infrastructure, with women's rights (women could be educated). If you look now at Iraq, Syria, and Libya, these countries are razed to the ground, bombed back to the Stone Age.

Creative Commons/E. Arrot

Jihadi fighters in Libya in 2011, who ripped the country apart, and signalled the Western drive for war against Russia and China.

These are the reasons for the refugees. If they are not discussed and corrected, then the problem will not be solved. We need this debate very urgently.

Since the military strike against Libya, the UN Security Council has been virtually nonfunctional. The Obama Administration has said that this was not a war but a "humanitarian intervention" to protect the poor rebels in Benghazi against the evil dictator Qaddafi. Of course it was still a military operation, but this lie at first convinced China and Russia to hold back; but to my knowledge, that was the last time they were taken in by such things.

The military strike against Libya was the point at which my husband Lyndon LaRouche, astute as he always is, said that there is a much larger purpose behind this: namely, to prepare for a thermonuclear war against Russia and China. At that time, many people said that simply cannot be, it's not possible; but now the people who deal with these things are no longer in doubt.

In September 2013, the war against Syria was almost at the point of a U.S. military strike, which was prevented literally in the last hours by the U.S. Chief of the Joint Chiefs of Staff, General Dempsey, who went to Obama at the White House and said: You have no mandate from Congress, and you will be impeached if you do it.

As already mentioned, in 2012 DIA director Gen. Michael Flynn had warned about the plans to build an Islamic Caliphate.

Catastrophic Situation in the U.S.

Does this mean that the United States is the beneficiary of this policy? Of course not. Former diplomats themselves such as Chas Freeman, former ambassador to Saudi Arabia and other countries, have given public speeches in Washington saying who said that even from the narrow perspective of American security interests, the U.S. has lost a massive amount of influence throughout the Middle East, because its enemies and the hatred of the United States have grown so enormously; this policy has been a total loss.

Has the United States itself profited economically? Not at all. The U.S. at the moment is in a classical breakdown crisis.

The *New York Times* reported last week that the mortality rate for white Americans between the ages of 40 and 50 has risen by 10%, and for the poor population even by 22% [from 1999 to 2014]. Forty or 50 is not a good age at which to die. With progressive medical research, people should live longer. The reason for this increase is alcoholism, drug abuse, and suicide. The number of drug-related deaths in the U.S. is now greater than the number of deaths from traffic accidents or firearms.

The official unemployment rate in America is about 5%, about 7.5 million. Ninety-four million people of working age are not included in the statistics. These are either people who have never had a job, or have given up looking for one, and are therefore no longer counted in the statistics. This adds up to 104 million Americans of working age who are unemployed, or 23%, about a quarter of the working-age population—an enormous loss for the economy. At the same time, people have to take on more work; they have a lower income and less free time.

Right now there is an escalating drug epidemic. In 2013, some 46,000 people died of an overdose: 120 per day. From 2007 to 2013, i.e., including during the Obama Administration, heroin addiction increased by 150%. For those with an annual income of $50,000 (about the median income), heroin consumption is up 60%. In New York, 60% of the people are at the poverty line or below. In Baltimore, one out of every ten people is addicted to heroin, and 50% of the people are functional illiterates.

Soldiers who deployed for several tours in Iraq and Afghanistan play an important role. Many come back with post-traumatic stress syndrome, and their families are completely destroyed.

The effect on the children is huge. Everyone knows the stories of shootings in schools and police violence which is the result of the militarization of the police—not as they are called in Germany "the police, your friend and helper;" they operate according to military principles, with military weapons.

The murder rate and violence in the African-American population is a whole chapter in itself. We recently had some guests who reported it to us in detail. It is a completely different world, a hell where "black on black crime" rules.

I could continue the list, but I do have to say for the sake of completeness that the next financial crash is imminent. There are several top economists who say it will likely happen before the end of the year. The IMF has just said we are unprepared for the next financial crisis, because all the instruments have already been used up. With the zero-interest-rate policy having been in effect for many years, it is impossible to lower rates

creative commons/Joshua Doubek

The crash of the commodity markets, especially oil, is devastating the one recent area of "growth" in the U.S. economy, the fracking industry, as shown here.

any further, and all countries are deeply in debt.

The commodity price bubble today is exactly what the housing bubble was in 2007, and will burst; the commercial real estate bubble is bigger today than in 2007; the "too-big-to-fail" banks are 40% bigger than in 2008; the total outstanding derivative debts are $2 quadrillion—i.e., $2,000 trillion. If that crashes, no bail-out and no bail-in will be enough.

For the United States it is absolutely clear: The only chance is to bankrupt Wall Street through Glass-Steagall. This is currently a very important topic in the election campaign, with Bernie Sanders and Martin O'Malley demanding it, and also Rand Paul on the Republican side, and the trade unions mobilizing for it. So the U.S. must reinstate Glass-Steagall, i.e., bank separation, and must become a republic again. This is the reason that my husband brought this process to Manhattan, to organize networks radiating out from Manhattan that will return the United States to its original character as a republic. This is an idea that is still endorsed by a minority, but there are also thinking Americans who look at the situation as I've just described it.

What Germany Can Do

What can Germany do in this situation? I have focussed so much on the strategic situation, because Germany is of course only a medium-sized country, and people always say: "We can't do anything anyway." But that is not the case at all. Germany can do very, very, very much.

1. The first step must be for a debate to be waged in Germany about what its existential interests actually are. Such a debate is completely lacking in the German media, it is lacking in German politics, and I can only ask you all to help us get this debate going.

Quite obviously it is not in the German interest to be cannon fodder for the imperialist plans to launch a third world war on behalf of an Anglo-American empire. In that case, there would be nothing left of Germany. Therefore, one of the first steps must be to end the sanctions against Russia immediately.

Helmut Schmidt recently said in an interview that the Ukraine crisis was not triggered by Russia's annexation of Crimea, but by the Maastricht Treaty. I can only fully and completely agree with the late Helmut Schmidt. That is the seed of the evil, because the Maastrich Treaty turned the EU into an empire, and the whole idea of expanding the EU eastward was born of exactly the same spirit as the eastward expansion of NATO. That was the reason that in November 2013, the EU presented Ukrainian President Viktor Yanukovych with a *fait accompli*, in the form of the EU Association Agreement, which Yanukovych then rejected at the last moment because it would simply not have worked. This was the beginning of the Maidan and everything that followed.

2. Secondly, I think that the participation of the Bundeswehr in all military operations that are part of this first strike scenario must be immediately ended. We in Germany must not take part in an offensive war. This is in the UN Charter; it was the self-evident reason for the Nuremberg trials, and war must never again emanate from German soil. As long as there are tactical nuclear weapons on German soil, this risk definitely remains.

3. We need a public debate on the security interests of all countries, including the security interests of

Russia and China. I have proposed for quite some time a new, inclusive, international security architecture. It must take into account the security interests of each country. Otherwise it is impossible to establish a peace order.

4. Fourthly, we need a public analysis and debate about the causes of the refugee crisis. I have already mentioned some points about that. Then Mr. Schäuble's ridiculous thesis about the inept skiers who triggered the avalanche can be tossed onto the garbage heap of history where it belongs. It was not an inept skier; it was precisely this policy of wars built upon lies and the support for rebels, where "good" rebels immediately turned into "bad" rebels, etc.

In addition, Mr. Schäuble should immediately resign, if he wants to contribute to a solution of the refugee crisis. His "black zero" (zero-deficit) policy, which has already plunged all of Southern Europe into disaster, which pushed Greece to the brink of the abyss, which has destroyed a third of the Greek economy, sending the suicide rate into the stratosphere, and sinking the people into despair—all this is the result of the black zero. If the black zero is now continued until 2016, even though dealing with the refugees obviously requires investment for which new loans must be made available, then what Mr. Schäuble says is the tinder, the fuel, that is stoking the escalation of right-wing violence in Germany. So Schäuble should resign.

5. I am for the immediate disbanding of the *Verfassungsschutz* and the BND. In their place, we should have a *German* intelligence service. Every country has the right to a secret service, but every country also has the right for its secret service to be of its own nationality.

6. Sixth, we should accept President Xi Jinping's offer to cooperate with the New Silk Road.

The Chinese Option

Here I must say very briefly: Luckily, in addition to these horrors that have developed in the trans-Atlantic world, there exists a very different economic model! China is at the center of it, but also the BRICS countries, which are now cooperating with many countries of Latin America, Asia, Eastern Europe, and Africa.

This economic model is based on entirely different principles. It is not a speculative casino economy, but is based on promotion of the common good. China developed its own economic model, which has achieved as much development in the past 30 years as the industrial countries in the past 200, as the focus was on excellence

Xinhua/Li Tao

Chinese President Xi Jinping (left), on his trip to Vietnam Nov. 5, toasts with Nguyen Phu Trong, General Secretary of the Communist Party of Vietnam.

in education, the utmost development of scientific and technological progress, and improving skills, in particular of the youth and women. China has also developed a new model of relations among nations, which calls for respect of the sovereignty of others, non-interference into their affairs, and acceptance of other social systems. Any country that wishes to join in the New Silk Road project is welcome to do so for the mutual benefit of all in a "win-win" strategy.

China is more Confucian than communist. China's 2,500 year old Confucian tradition is a defining factor in the entire political and economic life of the country. It is based, among other things, on an image of man as being unlimitedly perfectible. Confucius says you have to do something new every day—never do what you already did yesterday. It's absolute innovation. That has led to China being able to free 600 million people from poverty in the past 30 years. That's why I have made the point that China has done more for human rights than all the representatives of the so-called Western "com-munity of values," who talk a lot about democracy and human rights, but do the opposite.

The British, of course, are clever and see the new signs of the times. When Xi Jinping was recently in the UK, they rolled out the red carpet for him and spoke of the dawning of a golden era of British-Chinese relations. They like to be the first to jump on the bandwagon of new developments.

But Angela Merkel also, when she was in China, insisted on a strategic partnership. In particular in science and hi-tech areas, cooperation should be consolidated. And a very important seminar on the New Silk Road just took place in Spain, where the director of China's most important development center said that the New Silk Road should become a Noah's Ark for all countries in need. That is absolutely correct.

Of course, China is pursuing its own interests, but it also always respects and promotes the interests of the other. This can indeed become a Noah's Ark for all countries that are in need.

Development against Terrorism

I immediately proposed, in line with a proposal I made in 2012, that the only way to fight terrorism is to extend the New Silk Road to the Middle East and Africa. These regions are so destroyed at this point, and not only the cultural heritage in Palmyra or all the infrastructure, but the livelihood of the people has been largely destroyed as well.

Let's assume that all the neighbors have a fundamental interest in putting an end to terrorism. Russia is tremendously threatened by it. After all, the head of ISIS is a Chechen, and the Chechens are closely linked to the Right Sector in Ukraine, and are also closely related to ISIS; it's all one network. China has the same interest, because of Xinjiang and the Uighurs. India has huge problems due to the influence of Saudi Wahhabism-Salafism among the Muslim population, but so also do Iran, Egypt, etc. If all the neighboring countries work together on this, and then others, such as Germany, Italy, France and even the U.S., all say: Together, we will implement a Marshall Plan for the Middle East....

We will build the World Land-bridge, we will take the entire region and declare war on the desert, we will develop new water resources through desalinization of sea water. We will create new water supplies through ionization of the humidity in the atmosphere, we will green the deserts, we will build infrastructure and new cities. And, by doing so, we will create an incentive for the young people in the Middle East, so they do not become jihadis, but want to have a future, to start a family, to become scientists and engineers.

That is the only way to overcome terrorism. Bombs cannot do it alone; we have to create an incentive at the same time for these people to have a future.

At the Vienna conference two weeks ago, China put that forth as the 4th point of its proposal, that the reconstruction of Syria must begin immediately. The projects should start in the areas where peace reigns, so that people who are now at war already see the peace dividend as an incentive to end the war.

The same is true, of course, for Africa. The situation in Africa is not just due to the impact of this war policy. The West is also to blame for decades of non-development under the conditionalities of the International Monetary Fund and the Green environmentalist policy. The WWF stopped most of the projects, such as dams, river regulations, etc., and thus contributed to the current poverty.

We need to extend the World Land-bridge into these regions, and then we can have hope that the new name for peace is development.

Changing the Culture

For all of this to work, we in Germany also need a complete change in our culture. We need a paradigm change. The majority of the population today is controlled from the outside. Either we accept living under a dictatorship or an oligarchy, under the motto "we can't do anything anyway"—which is the most common phrase heard among Germans—or we just go along. We accept the entertainment industry and stupidities on television.

I don't know if you watch TV, but all you can find now are crime series. There are no more movies. Recently the "Movie of the Week" was running, and I turned on the TV with joy. What was it? A crime thriller! This is a real dumbing-down, as if the whole world were made up of crimes, how to solve them, and the odd relationships among police captains.

There has been an incredible dumbing-down of intellectual life. There is no cultural debate, no intellectual fights over about the great issues of our time.

If Germany is to survive this difficult historical

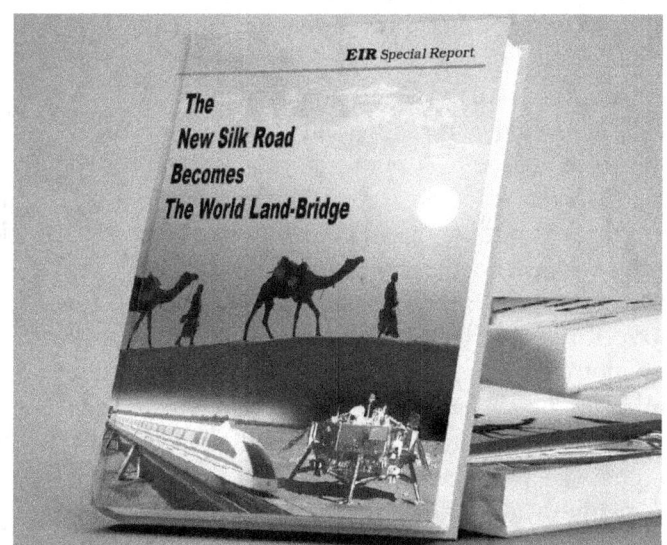

moment, we must re-discover our true identity. What I mean by true identity is, of course, Classical culture. Classical culture as it was developed in music, through Bach, Schubert, Mozart, Beethoven, Schumann, Brahms. In terms of poetry, we are just as richly blessed, with Lessing, Schiller, Heine, and hundreds of other classical poets. In philosophy and natural sciences, as is known, Germany is the country which has produced the most thinkers, poets, discoverers and inventors, but they are just not known any more. Who reads Nicholas of Cusa, Kepler, Leibniz? Who knows Schiller's poems by heart or who applies the aesthetic theory in everyday life?

We have to get to know these classical figures once again and then refuse such outside control over our minds, because that is what determines the "good conduct" of the conformist, which says we want to belong to a certain group, a certain club, the trans-Atlantic club or the free-market club or some other club which is supposed to be advantageous for us. That is why we are not free.

The reason we are unfree is not because Germany has not signed a peace treaty, as some people repeat endlessly. We are not free because we do not have inner freedom. We have to find our way back to an inner control, to self-determination. What Schiller says in his wonderful poem "Hope"—"what the inner voice speaks"—is true, and that is what we must learn to hear again.

My husband has recently talked about "placement" of the voice in *bel canto* singing and its importance. The Italian *bel canto* method, the "art of beautiful singing," has to do with putting the voice in the right place. That implies considering the entire human body, chest voice, head voice, all the resonance chambers of the body, as pieces of one instrument, and apprehending there the intonation and intention of the composer. But it does not just involve "placing" the notes or the music; it actually concerns tuning our lives, and the placement of our identity within the order of creation.

Anyone who has already considered whether there is really such a thing as a premonition,—and this is not just to be understood in a religious way, or according to any one religion. Most of you have already experienced the sentiment one has when one does exactly what is necessary to do. When you know that you are acting as

creative commons

The monument to poets Wolfgang Goethe and Friedrich Schiller in Weimar, Germany.

a "good Samaritan," that you as a person are acting, essentially, in a human way, in the way one should actually always act, but unfortunately only manages to do so from time to time. But everyone knows this sentiment of inner happiness or inner freedom, where you know that you freely doing what's necessary. That is the quality of inner freedom that we have to win back.

Schiller described this in his demands of an artist. He said that before an artist dares to move his public, he must first ennoble himself to the level of an ideal person. We have to make the same demand on ourselves. Not that we will manage to do it every second and every minute, but we act on the idea that we achieve our own humanity, by contributing, through our living, something which allows mankind to progress.

That is actually what should define us. That is what German culture must re-become.

This speech was translated from the German.

Philippines Revolts Against Obama's War on China

Nov. 16 (EIRNS)—A revolutionary change is taking place in the Philippines, threatening to collapse President Obama's mad drive for nuclear confrontation with China. That plan, first launched as Obama's "Pivot to Asia" in 2012, involves shifting expanded naval, air, and land forces to Asia, along with enhanced ballistic missile defense systems, in a ring around China and the Russian Far East.

Most importantly, it includes Obama's plan to re-occupy the Philippines militarily with the most advanced naval, air, and ground forces and military equipment.

Now, faced with Russian President Putin's brilliant flanking action against Obama's war policy in Europe and the Middle East—by waging an effective war on ISIS in cooperation with the Syrian government and others—Obama has responded by focussing with a vengeance on his policy of war against China.

Obama and his subservient President of the Philippines, Benigno "Noynoy" Aquino, are attempting to circumvent the Philippine Constitution, which, since 1991, has explicitly forbidden the presence of any foreign military bases on Philippine soil. Their ploy is to pretend that the new U.S. bases are not bases at all, but will be set up within Philippine military bases, with the Americans declared to be merely "guests."

Aquino further claims that the Enhanced Defense Cooperation Agreement (EDCA) which enables this charade, is not a treaty, but only an "executive agreement," and thus does not require the approval of the Philippine Senate, as required by law for such a treaty.

Xinhua/Rouelle Umali

Philippine President Benigno Aquino (right) greets Chinese Foreign Minister Wang Yi at the presidential palace in Manila Nov. 10, 2015.

Fortunately, this scam is falling apart, thanks to a series of actions and interventions by patriots of the Philippines, joined by American patriots who recognize the threat of global thermonuclear war inherent in Obama's confrontation with China. These actions, documented below, include:

• A declaration by Filipinos in Solidarity for Sovereignty (PINAS)—which has also taken the EDCA to the Supreme Court on constitutional grounds—saying that the recent U.S. military provocations against Chinese territories in the South China Sea bring the world to the brink of war, and exemplify why the Philippines must reject the U.S. military occupation.

• A friend of the court (Petition for Intervention) brief by U.S. Senator Mike Gravel (Alaska 1969-81) to the Philippine Supreme Court, arguing on moral, historical, and political grounds that the re-occupation of the Philippines must be stopped.

• A call by Philippine Senator Kit Tatad (1992-2001) for the Philippines to declare official neutrality.

• A dramatic vote in the Philippine Senate on November 9, passing a resolution by a vote of 15-1 that declares that the EDCA is indeed a treaty and must be approved by the Senate. The resolution—brought by Senator Miriam Defensor-Santiago, a presidential candidate for the 2016 election—pre-empted the the the Supreme Court, which had leaked that its decision would approve the EDCA and would be released on November 16, the day before President Obama is scheduled to arrive in the Philippines for the annual APEC Summit.

Obama's effort to be ordained the new governor-general of a colonial Philippines has been thwarted, thus far.

Revolt Across Asia

These developments in the Philippines come at a time when the rest of Asia is also reacting against Obama's war drive. A meeting of the defense ministers of the 10 members of the Association of Southeast Asian Nations (ASEAN) plus the United States, China, Japan, and others, on Nov. 13 in Kuala Lumpur, Malaysia, rejected Obama's demand, delivered by U.S. Secretary of Defense Ashton Carter, that the final communiqué denounce China for "aggression" in the South China Sea. No communiqué was issued as a result.

In fact, China's President Xi Jinping on Nov. 6 visited Vietnam—one of the countries Obama has encouraged to denounce Chinese "aggression" in the South China Sea—and the two nations re-established strong strategic ties. Then Chinese Foreign Minister Wang Yi visited Manila to prepare for President Xi's visit for the APEC Summit. President Aquino promised that the South China Sea issue would not be on the APEC agenda.

The ASEAN members naturally want to be part of China's New Silk Road projects for real development, rather than Obama's anti-China alliance. But they also increasingly recognize that the militarization of the region is not coming from China, which is only building up islands already under their control, but from Obama, whose plan for at least eight U.S. military bases in the Philippines even includes two in the South China Sea, on Palawan Island—and they want no part of it.

LaRouche's Role

In several of these developments, friends of Lyndon LaRouche are playing a crucial role. In their own words, here is the documentation of the courageous steps taken by citizens of a small nation to prevent the madness of a global thermonuclear war, and to demand development as the basis for peace.

Is Neutrality an Option for the Philippines?

by Francisco S. Tatad

Nov. 16—The following (edited) op-ed in the Manila Times *was written by Francisco "Kit" Tatad, Minister of Public Information under President Ferdinand Marcos from 1969 to 1980, and Senator of the Philippines from 1992 to 2001. Sen. Tatad is a founding member of the National Transformation Council.*

The Prospect of War

WASHINGTON, Nov. 13 (EIRNS)—Given the maritime conflict between China and Japan, between China and the Philippines, and America's concern over China's conduct in the disputed areas, armed hostilities could arise between China on the one hand, and the United States and Japan on the other, with the Philippines probably absorbing some of the missiles. This is the fear of some Filipino analysts I have met here.

...The Philippines is not militarily prepared for any war, but by talking like it very badly needs to take on the Asian hegemon, the Aquino regime may have created a situation nobody wants or is ready for....

The Idea of Being Neutral

One analyst, who asked that I withhold his name, has proposed one such unthinkable question. Given the growing rivalry between the United States and China, and the distinct possibility that we might get caught in the middle, if and when it explodes into a

Philippine Senator Francisco (Kit) Tatad, addressing a conference of the Save the Nation movement, founded by Philippines LaRouche Society leader Butch Valdes, in April 2013.

Can a country like the Philippines offer a solution? This is what the analyst wanted me to explore. The Philippines is one of China's oldest trading partners, and at the same time, a historic U.S. military and political ally. It should be a friend to both sides....

Until 1975, when Marcos established diplomatic relations with Beijing, the Chinese Communist Party was said to be funding, training, and arming the New People's Army (NPA) and the Communist Party of the Philippines (CPP). The cessation of Chinese support for the CPP/NPA was one of the conditions for Marcos' recognition of Beijing. On the other hand, military assistance and security support came solely from the United States, with which the Philippines had a Mutual Defense Treaty signed in 1950 (and in force until now), and a military bases agreement, signed in 1947 and ending in 1991.

violent confrontation, can neutrality be an option for the Philippines? It is not easy to formulate this question, for obvious reasons. Because of our longstanding security alliance with the United States, just to ask the question already carries with it the smell of treason....

Why neutrality? Because the analyst's fear is that an air-sea battle could erupt in our disputed waters, and it would not be easy to remain a non-belligerent then. He does not see hostilities being limited to a small war solely between China and the Philippines on account of their maritime territorial dispute. The issue has been there since the 1950s, and only during the presidency of B.S. Aquino III did it become a serious bilateral problem.

Imagining War

The analyst believes that, were real hostilities to occur, they are more likely to be between the United States and Japan on the one hand, and China on the other, because of the larger question of regional dominance and sphere of influence. As the oldest Asia-Pacific power and the world's only superpower, the United States, with its Seventh Fleet, is not likely to give up its historic role. But China is now a world economic power, and a rising regional military power, and will not want to be elbowed out of its own natural theatre....

U.S.-Philippine Security Ties

When the bases agreement expired in 1991, the United States tried to negotiate a new treaty extending the bases by another 10 years. This was shot down by the Senate in 1992, despite President Corazon Aquino's frenzied effort to win Senate approval. This chilled Philippine-U.S. relations for a while until the two governments entered into a Visiting Forces Agreement in 1999. As Senate Majority Leader at the time, I co-sponsored the Senate resolution concurring in its ratification.

In 2014, the Aquino government signed an Enhanced Defense Cooperation Agreement (EDCA) with the United States without the participation of the Senate. The Constitution provides that after 1991, foreign military bases, troops, or facilities shall not be allowed in the Philippines except under a treaty duly concurred in by the Senate and, when the Congress so requires, ratified by a majority of the votes cast by the people in a national referendum held for that purpose, and recognized as a treaty by the other contracting state.

The EDCA does not create any new bases, but allows the United States to deploy its troops and facilities inside any Philippine military establishment. It also allows nuclear vessels to come and go as they please, despite the constitutional ban on nuclear weapons in the country. All this seems consistent with Aquino's support for President Obama's pivot to Asia.

Undoing What Aquino Has Done

Aquino's handling of the nation's foreign and national security policies has created a situation that needs to be undone.... The Philippines needs to compose its own differences with China, instead of getting involved in any quarrel that is not its own. It should try to promote friendship and cooperation between China and the United States, instead of getting caught in the middle of any possible confrontation. How can this be done? The analyst suggests either a non-aggression pact with China or a state of neutrality for the Philippines. This, he points out, is consistent with the Philippine constitutional provision which renounces war as an instrument of national policy.

U.S. Neutrality

With respect to neutrality, he points to the early American experience. In 1793, he recalls, President George Washington issued a proclamation of neutrality, which enabled his young nation to avoid the war raging between France and England. The United States was militarily weak at the time, and fighting a war would have endangered its very existence. This enabled the United States to grow from inside, so that by 1823, it was strong enough to proclaim the Monroe Doctrine, which warned the European powers that further efforts to colonize land or interfere with states in North or South America would be regarded as acts of aggression, requiring U.S. intervention.

From 1935 to 1939, President Roosevelt invoked the Neutrality Act again and again to avoid getting embroiled in the European wars.... On Dec. 8, 1941, the United States declared war on Japan, a day after it had attacked Pearl Harbor. On Dec. 11, 1941, Germany and Italy declared war on the United States, and on the same day the United States responded with similar declarations. By now the United States had become a great war power, but for as long as it lasted, its neutrality had a glorious run.

Some Rights and Duties of Neutrals

Under the Hague Convention of 1907, the territory of neutral powers is inviolable.

Library of Congress

President George Washington declared U.S. neutrality in the midst of the great European conflicts of the 1790s.

Belligerents are forbidden to move troops, or convoys of either war munitions or supplies, across the territory of a neutral power. They are likewise forbidden to (a) erect on the territory of a neutral power a wireless telegraphy station or other apparatus for the purpose of communicating with belligerents on land or sea, or (b) use any installation of this kind established by them before the war on the territory of a neutral power for purely military purposes, and which has not been opened for the service of public messages.

Corps of combatants cannot be formed nor recruiting agencies opened on the territory of a neutral power to assist the belligerents.

A neutral power has the right and the duty to resist any attempt to violate its neutrality, even by force, without [being regarded as] committing a hostile act....

Effects of Neutrality

Were the Philippines to become neutral, it would remove itself from the center of the evolving conflict between China on the one hand, and the United States and Japan on the other. It would also allow a policy of equidistance from the competing Asia-Pacific powers. This would enable it to develop an independent world view and a foreign policy that looks primarily to its own interests, rather than to those of its external patrons. For the first time in its history, it would be compelled to stand on its own. This would not be without pain in the beginning, but if Switzerland provides any inspiration, the end result could be rewarding. It would allow the country to nourish and fulfill its own ambitions.

But it would mean dismantling the U.S.-Philippine alliance which has helped to undergird the U.S. security system in the Asia-Pacific region until now. Do you believe there is anyone on the horizon who would risk his chance of becoming president by suggesting to Washington that this is one great idea whose time has come?
—fstatad@gmail.com

PINAS Statement on U.S. Actions Hostile to the Philippines

Nov. 16—The following statement was issued by Filipinos in Solidarity for Sovereignty (PINAS) on the U.S. provocation in the South China Sea and the planned U.S. military occupation of Philippine bases. It was drafted by Butch Valdes, the head of the Philippine LaRouche Society, and adopted by PINAS on Oct. 30. PINAS also brought the case against EDCA to the Supreme Court.

Despite our presently unresolved territorial issues with countries surrounding the West Philippine Seas, it is with unequivocal opposition that we view the outrageous military provocation of China by U.S. President Obama under the guise of freedom of navigation.

In blatant disregard for the sovereignty and security concerns of Southeast Asian Nations, the U.S. has initiated threatening actions against China, which not only destabilize the whole region, but also may provide the

Antonio 'Butch' Valdes, addressing the Schiller Institute New Paradigm conference of June 2103 in San Francisco by video.

spark of thermonuclear confrontation between the two superpowers.

Our concern is aggravated by the declared and insane acquiescence of the current President, Benigno Aquino III, in the critically dangerous advances by an equally impaired Barack Obama. The risk to 100 million Filipino lives notwithstanding, Aquino has signed a constitutionally infirm agreement allowing the U.S. forces to have access to all our airports and seaports, ply our territorial waters, and set up American bases within our Philippine bases.

It is this highly questionable accommodation by the Philippine President, and the tacit approval of a mercenary Senate and an obviously intimidated Supreme Court, that has provided U.S. nuclear-armed warships the bases to mount and implement provocative action against their principal adversary in the region.

We call on all patriotic Filipinos to *reject* the presently disastrous condition of allowing foreign military installations in Philippine territories. The U.S. geopolitical intentions, through President Obama's actions, are manifestly clear. Their decisions and actions in Iraq, Afghanistan, Libya, Yemen, Egypt, Syria, and Ukraine are now glaring examples of internal chaos, *after* they have been supposedly liberated from dictatorship, into democracy.

Let us uphold the principles of sovereignty, and advocate a world community of Sovereign Nation-States—bound by a common objective—to improve the quality of life of every single human being on the planet, so that our generation and those after us, can reap the benefits of Man's collaboration and collective creativity.

The Philippines Must Save Itself, And Help Save Us From Ourselves

U.S. Senator Mike Gravel (D-AK 1969-81) filed the following (slightly edited) Friend of the Court brief (called Petition for Intervention in the Philippines) in the Supreme Court of the Philippines on November 10, 2015, in the case challenging the constitutionality of the EDCA.

Summary

The decision by the Philippine government to enter into an Enhanced Defense Cooperation Agreement (EDCA) with the United States government is neither in the best interest of the Philippine people nor in the best interest of the American people.

Nizar Abboud

Former Senator Mike Gravel speaking to the UN Press Correspondents in New York City, Sept. 14, 2015.

Throughout human history, conflicts that develop between national empires in decline ceding status and power to ascending nations have invariably led to war. This occurrence is what General Martin Dempsey, the former chairman of the Joint Chiefs of Staff, called the Thucydides trap, in which Athenian fear of a rising Sparta made the Peloponnesian War inevitable. It is noteworthy that it was the democratic Athens that initiated the war, not the autocratic Sparta. Fortunately, there are some instances in history in which precarious superpower transitions have not led to war. China's ascendancy is primarily economic in nature, and no evidence suggests that it seeks global military hegemony even though its economic interests are global. To the contrary, China's military expenditures in response to the irresponsible rhetoric of

some American leaders have increased over the last decade, but are still considerably less than a third of United States annual military expenditures, which amount equals half the world's total military expenditures.

President Obama's recent speech before the UN General Assembly quieted the chamber when he articulated the following threat:

> I lead the strongest military that the world has ever known, and I will never hesitate to protect my country or our allies, unilaterally and by force where necessary.

… I will argue below that the United States, whether intentionally or by accident, is skirting ever so close to the Thucydides trap. America's political leadership is unable to reverse that trajectory. Therefore, it is my hope that a foreign national interest will step forward to protect Americans from their own government's military foreign policies.

The Philippines could possibly take up a portion of that task, and in so doing, safeguard its own sovereign interests while avoiding military engagements and a possible war that no one wants. The decision of this esteemed Supreme Court can set in motion a chain of circumstances that could have an impact on whether the conflict caused by China's global economic ascendency and the loss of United States hegemonic mili-

The result of falling for the Thucydides trap: The Peloponnesian War between Athens and Sparta, 431-404 BC.

tary primacy in the Indo-Pacific economic center of gravity, will result in war by falling into the Thucydides trap.

Credentials

We are most critical of what we hold most dear. I love my country, but I cannot abide the concept 'my country right or wrong.' When it is wrong, I hope to propound an effective critique to negate that wrong. As a young man, I enlisted in the United States Army and graduated from the Infantry School's Officer Candidate Program at Fort Benning, Georgia. Most of my class went to Korea at the worst of the fighting. I had the good fortune, having been educated by the Army as a Counter Intelligence Corps (CIC) agent, of being sent to Europe as the Adjutant of the Communications Intelligence Service, an agency that used the CIC as its cover. As a 23-year-old second lieutenant, I had the authority to classify and declassify military documents.

Advancing 20 years, little wonder that, as a 41-year-old U.S. Senator, I instantly accepted the responsibility from Daniel Ellsberg of officially releasing the Pentagon Papers, top secret documents that revealed the history of how four presidential administrations, and later a fifth, had lied to the American people about the reasons for our involvement in the quagmire of the Vietnam War. The Nixon Administration's Justice Department sought my indictment, occasioning a case that was unanimously decided by the U.S. Supreme Court

that a member of Congress could reveal any classified information within the confines of the Congress without being questioned by any other authority under the provisions of the speech and debate clause of the U.S. Constitution....

As a legislator, I served as a representative and Speaker of the Alaska House of Representatives (1963-1966) and served two terms in the U.S. Senate representing the people of Alaska (1969-1981). Politically, I had the honor of enjoying the full electoral support of the Alaskan Philippine community. During my Senate career I had occasion to visit the Philippines as the guest of Ferdinand Marcos—a visit I found most instructive.

Since I was committed to the enactment of the Law of the Sea and played a leadership role in seeking its ratification in the Senate, I was appointed the delegate from the U.S. Senate to the 31st General Assembly of the United Nations.

As I stated above, I love my country, however, I hold my love of mankind above that of my country. I hold the life of any human being equal to that of any American.

I pray this distinguished Court will find the above credentials sufficient to warrant your attention to the views I express in this paper.

History

History forgotten is often repeated. Please keep in the forefront of your deliberations the history of the United States as it impacted the Philippines and the peoples of Southeast Asia. Understanding this history will clarify what possible effects the EDCA could have on the Philippine people.

As you know, after several centuries of Spanish colonial rule, the Katipunan revolt began in 1892 and was formalized with the Filipino War of Independence in 1896. Most of America's media attention centered on Cuba. When the United States declared war against Spain in 1898, the congressional declaration included the Teller Amendment, which disclaimed any intention of the United States to annex Cuba, and promised to leave the island as soon as the war was over. No such declaratory reservation was made with respect to the Philippine archipelago, also in a revolt against Spain.

In one spectacular battle, Admiral George Dewey destroyed the entire Spanish fleet bottled up in Manila Bay. He then invited Emilio Aguinaldo to return from exile to prosecute a land war against the Spanish—American ground troops had yet to arrive—with the inducement of prospective independence for a Philippine Republic.

Henceforth, a duplicitous manipulation ensued involving all of the usual suspects: the U.S. President, the State Department, the Congress, the Navy, the Army, the jingoistic American media, and the ill-informed patriotic American public, oblivious to the trashing of its most fundamental values: liberty, freedom, national sovereignty, and self-determination.

From such *realpolitik* stagecraft under the administrations of William McKinley, Theodore Roosevelt, and Woodrow Wilson evolved a crushing insurgent war on the Philippine population, exhibiting a level of cruelty and atrocity equal to the worst in the annals of conquest and war. The result: All opposition was brutally crushed and the Filipino leadership and population remained supine to American interests, except for a brief interlude commencing on September 16, 1991.

At the Treaty of Paris, December 10, 1898, ending the Spanish-American War, Spain would not involve the lowly revolutionaries of Cuba or the Philippines in the surrender process, to which the U.S. did not object. In the treaty, Spain renounced its rights to Cuba, acknowledging its independence, ceded Puerto Rico and the island of Guam to the United States, and sold the Philippines to the United States for $20,000,000. The sale afforded a level of legitimacy to the U.S. ownership of the archipelago because of the earlier purchase of Alaska from Russia.

It was not until the presidential administration of Franklin Roosevelt in 1934 that the right of Filipino self-determination was acknowledged with a promise of independence—delayed until 1946, after the end of World War II, during which Filipino fighters acquitted themselves with courage and resolve equal to that of any nation.

Perley Fremont Rockett/Library of Congress

The brutal Philippine-American War of the late Nineteenth-early Twentieth Century.

...Add to this limited recitation of past facts the criminal complicity that the United States foisted on the Philippines with the prosecution of wars against fellow South Asians. I am not only referring to our conduct in Indochina, but also to the wanton invasions of Cambodia, Laos, and the corruption of Thailand. Subic Bay and Clark Air Base were the main platforms outside the war zone to supply military resources to American forces to prosecute the Vietnam War in a manner not dissimilar to the pacification of the insurgent war pursued against the Philippine population at the turn of the century.

We need to remember that a commander of the American Air Force advocated the use of nuclear weapons to bomb the Vietnamese into submission—in effect depopulating the country to save it from going communist. We should also remember that during the Korean War General Douglas MacArthur, the son of General Arthur MacArthur who figured prominently in the suppression of the Philippine insurgency, advocated the use of nuclear weapons in Korea and on China. It is not unfair to conclude that some Western elites placed little value on Asian lives.

Even to this day, a significant leader in Congress and a former presidential candidate still believes that we should have won the Vietnam War, and that we only failed for lack of political resolve. That war was never winnable, for the Vietnamese were prepared to pay any price to become an independent sovereign nation.

When we decamped under pressure because of American protests at home, we left many of our Asian allies at the mercy of the enemies we had created for them. We also left a refugee crisis—boat people—that had some impact on the Philippines. At the height of the war, America's leaders knew it was a mistake and had long given up on the Domino Theory. They were only concerned with a face-saving exit.

Nevertheless, our global reputation was damaged. As a result, we punished the people of Southeast Asia with sanctions and trade embargoes for a generation.

The truth of this history, so hard to accept, is that the millions of Filipinos, Indo-Chinese, Laotians, Cambodians, and Americans all died in vain.

The political ideology of communism we so abhorred still exists, but now Vietnam enjoys most favored trade status with America. They did die in vain. There is no question that the Philippines benefited economically from America's war in Southeast Asia. However, I would maintain that the moral price and the militarization of the Filipino culture was far too high a price to pay.

The phenomena of this interlude in history baffle many Americans. We don't know why these people, who have been so abused by us, have forgiven us and still greet us with amity. Do they not understand what we have done?

China

...The U.S. agitation over the Spratly Islands created by China dredging and building up reefs has great propaganda value for America. However, the charge that they are military bases is somewhat specious. A military base presupposes that it would play some useful operational role in the event of hostilities. Physically these small islands are easily destroyed in the event of a conflict and therefore are not military bases in any sense of the word. These islands are outposts of a symbolic nature—markers that would enhance legal arguments for rights at some future date.

However, from a Philippine and Chinese perspec-

courtesy of South Sea Conversations via New Sohu.com

A section of the Scarborough Shoal in the South China Sea, a source of simmering conflict between the Philippines and China. Here a Philippines member of parliament leads military and media personnel to the Shoal in May 1997.

tive, these disputes are serious. Filipino fishermen make their living fishing these waters, and the economic benefits from prospective oil and gas discoveries could be significant. The solutions to these disputes, not only for the Philippines but for all the interested nations in the region, are best dealt with diplomatically under the auspices of the United Nations and not by military confrontations.

In the Scarborough Reef incident, China confronted Filipino fishermen over their access to the reef. Even though the United States got involved, the Filipinos were forced to back down. This successful incident in 2012 suggests a policy for China to go it alone in the South China Sea. It offers a model for continued Chinese confrontations, nibbling at the margins of the national interests of the Philippines, Malaysia, Taiwan, Indonesia, and Vietnam.

At present, the issue rests with the International Tribunal for the Law of the Sea. I would hope that the tribunal would use its influence to initiate a UN regional forum, inviting all the interested parties to treat these sovereignty issues from a broader perspective than that of any one single party. This should have appeal to China, which has advantaged economically all parties in the region with its spectacular global growth. This forum would permit China to showcase its Silk Road—One Belt, One Road—vision by including the disputants in the economic vision with specific development projects, and thereby advance harmony by sharing the commons of the China Sea.

The Scarborough Reef incident should inform the Philippine leadership that when push turns to shove, the United States will not provoke a military showdown with China over Filipino fishing or mineral rights. It should drive home the fact that U.S. militarization of the Philippines is not really designed to protect Philippine interests but rather to afford the United States a geographic advantage to confront China over its ascendant superpower status, which the United States finds offensive to its global hegemonic status.

It is somewhat disingenuous for the United States to claim that it is patrolling the South China Sea to protect the right of free maritime passage when the United States is one of very few nations that refuse to ratify the Law of the Sea (LOS) convention, which expressly codified in international law the protection of the oceans environment, its fisheries, the sovereign rights of bordering nations, and free maritime passage, and provides a tribunal to adjudicate maritime disputes under the convention.

My personal assessment of China is not that of America's conventional wisdom. When President Obama praised the UN record during its 70-year existence for raising more than a billion people out of poverty into the middle class, he failed to mention that half of that number were Chinese. It was done in three decades—a record of human improvement never equaled in the recorded annals of civilization. China is not a democracy, but a communist country operating as a meritocracy, struggling to limit corruption, a vice endemic to free-market capitalism. China's accomplishment in improving the wellbeing of more than 500,000,000 people in a generation—a number more than one and a half times the entire population of the United States—should have been noted by the American president.

The governance problems that China faces, and for that matter that India and Indonesia face, are almost beyond comprehension. I do not pretend to know the nuanced relationship that existed between China and the Philippines over the last century, but I am sure some degree of fraternity must exist over the shared experience of colonial exploitation. That would be enough to build upon.

I am not suggesting that the Philippines alienate itself from the United States, but I think it wise to divorce itself from any military entanglements, whether with the United States, Japan, the European Union, or China. Is there a threat of invasion from China or from any other nation against the Philippines? If not, then why the fascination with taking on the burden of militarism, and why pay for wasteful munitions when those monies can better be used to improve the life of Filipinos?

China, supported by the BRICS—Brazil, Russia, India, China and South Africa—has defined a 30-year vision, already undertaken, to unite the world's economies through the construction of high-speed railroads, roads, and fiber optic communications across the Eurasian land mass of Russia from western China to Europe, with extensions north into Scandinavian countries and south into Iran and Arab countries. This visionary plan makes good sense for China, which must productively utilize the excess industrial capacity it developed for its double-digit economic growth.

The Silk Road—One Belt, One Road—plan has a maritime component to build efficient port developments to increase world trade. The plan envisions a similar economic expansion to all continents. Hegemonic influences will not be tolerated, nor will it have a military component. The BRICS have already set up financial institutions to help underwrite developments undertaken by the plan. Embarrassingly, America tried to dissuade its allies, without success, from participating in the plan.

It would be a tremendous boon to the Philippine economy to avoid the American military expansion and instead join the BRICS in this sensible global economic development plan. The Philippines, India, and China are not included in the U.S.-led Trans-Pacific Partnership (TPP), which serves to add greater power to the multinational corporations who already control major portions of the world economy. This agreement is the U.S. strategy to confront the BRICS global economic alignment. In my view, it makes more sense for the Philippines to align itself with the BRICS and eschew the militarism offered by the United States.

Compare China's vision for a successful, prosperous, economically unified world to what America offers by way of a militarized world that brooks no challenge to its hegemonic leadership. Compare the suffering of untold numbers of people in a plethora of nations around the world over the last 30 years. A suffering inflicted by the hubris of backroom American neocons punishing people with economic sanctions to bring about regime change and their liberal interventionists wantonly invading sovereign nations that do not conform to their ideological standards.

Save Yourselves

...The United States is attempting to make the Philippines the sharpened point of its offensive spear with which to confront China. Ultimately, Filipinos will find themselves impaled on that spear. The Philippines is the ideal strategic location for the United States to establish a military platform in East Asia, on China's doorstep, in preparation for a possible war.

Chinese Navy unofficial spokesman Admiral Yin Zhuo (PLA Navy ret.) made the point recently: "If in the future, there is U.S.-China conflict, then it will likely take place on our doorstep. Speaking bluntly, fighting on our doorstep, we fear no one." The doorstep he is referring to is the Philippines.

The U.S. design on Philippine real estate is understandable. The more confusing question: Why would any country choose to place itself at the frictional edge of the world's two conflicting superpowers? If there is a war, the conventional phase of it would first be fought on Philippine soil housing the American military, before moving to the nuclear phase of the war on the Chinese and American populations, in which case we are all doomed.

Unfortunately, many American civilian and military leaders, intoxicated with the sense of superiority they feel towards the rest of the world, tend to miscalculate in their political and military planning.... The vaunted nuclear carrier armadas the United States boasts of to protect its Asian allies—most particularly the Philippines—can be wiped out in minutes with anti-ship ballistic missiles and a plethora of China's new classes of advanced supersonic cruise missiles.

What could possibly be the benefit for the Philippines of turning itself over to a foreign power? Because that will be the case if the EDCA stands. Your country will be garrisoned to the hilt in order to back up America's threats to anyone in Asia. Take a look at the neighborhoods around military bases to see what your country will become. Who other than military contractors would dare invest and develop alternate industries in such a circumstance? The economic activities that will follow military expansion will of necessity control and corrupt your political institutions to protect their investments. The government would prostitute itself to a foreign power and will then demand payments. However, such payments would be a pittance compared to what could be realized from the normal growth of a healthy, independent economy blessed with an industrious people.

Save Us from Ourselves

As an American, realistic enough to understand the internal dilemma that afflicts my country, I sincerely ask for the help of this illustrious Court by taking a decision that could set in motion a chain of circumstances that could possibly thwart the planned expansion of America's military presence in Asia, using the Philippines as its main base. This is what some call the pivot to Asia. Let me explain why it is impossible for some of us to alter or correct the present direction of our foreign and military policy.

Our culture is infused with a sense of superiority, enlarged beyond reality. Our nation was blessed by geography providing oceanic security, by a land welling up with vast resources, and an ever-expanding educated and industrious population. After France midwifed our nation's birth, we saw ourselves as the city on the hill, with a manifest destiny to transcend the continent.

Of course, we rarely acknowledge that we are a violent people who annihilated the indigenous population of the continent and institutionalized slavery in our Constitution, only to have it corrected by a calamitous Civil War, which left a legacy of racism that haunts us to this day at home and abroad. The seeds of hubris grew when we saved the world in the Second World War, while the communist Soviet Union did the heavy lifting. This left us as the only imperial power with the atomic bomb able to assume the white man's burden from the British Empire. The acquisition of the bomb by the USSR and China altered that equation.

After the war, our elites reasoned that we could avoid another terrible depression if we kept the economy on a war footing. This policy was legislated into existence in 1947 with the National Security Act under the Truman administration and carried forward by the

Eisenhower administration. The military-industrial complex reasoned that if it located the military's economic presence—manufacturing and military bases—in every congressional district, it could control the Congress. And it has....

The U.S. Empire is in decline even though we still lead the European Union and North Asia around by the nose. NATO, 90% funded by the United States and commanded by an American general, is the vehicle for the globalization of the military-industrial complex. American leadership and the public refuse to accept the fact of decline. You need but look at our failing educational system, our health system controlled by the insurance industry, our bankrupt financial system, and the disrepair of our national infrastructure. In the face of all this, the defense budget remains sacrosanct. The American public is not stupid, but remains steeped in ignorance by a mainstream media controlled by six corporations responsible to Wall Street and the military-industrial complex.

We are no longer a democracy in the real sense of the word. A democracy is not just elections. For elections to be meaningful, people must be informed in order to render intelligent judgment. The American public is purposely kept in ignorance.

American political and military diplomacy is contriving to gain control of your archipelago for reasons that will not benefit the people who live there.

Conclusion

...The discussion above is made in an attempt to motivate this distinguished Court to render a judicial decision that will in effect transfer the deliberations on the EDCA from its secret confines to the Philippine Senate, where arguments will be made in full public view. I hope my arguments made above will contribute to that debate. Matters of extreme importance to the wellbeing of Filipinos and the survivability of Philippine democracy are at stake in that debate.

Your judicial decision could well set a chain of circumstances in motion that could ultimately affect the course of world affairs. In this regard, I am reminded of a famous statement made by the renowned sociologist Margaret Mead: Never doubt that a small group of thoughtful, committed citizens can change the world; indeed, it's the only thing that ever has.

by Mike Gravel
October 15, 2015